WALTER OSBORNE

Walter Osborne

Jeanne Sheehy

The National Gallery of Ireland

Exhibition held at

THE NATIONAL GALLERY OF IRELAND
16 November — 31 December 1983

THE ULSTER MUSEUM, BELFAST
20 January — 29 February 1984

British Library Cataloguing in Publication Data
Sheehy, Jeanne
    Walter Osborne
    1. Osborne, Walter — Exhibition
    I. Title   II. Osborne, Walter
    III. National Gallery of Ireland
    IV. Ulster Museum
    The National Gallery of Ireland, 1983
    759.2'915   ND497.0/

ISBN   0-903162-09-1

Design, typesetting and origination by
Printset & Design Ltd.
Printed by Ormond Printing Co. Ltd.

Cover: *The House Builders* (detail)

Frontispiece: *Walter Osborne painting the
portrait of Thomas W. Moffett, President,
Queen's College, Galway.* (National Gallery of Ireland
Cat. No. 601).

Contents

Abbreviations

Cat. No.   Catalogue number
H.R.H.A.   Honorary Member, Royal Hibernian Academy
I.P.O.C.   Institute of Painters in Oil Colours
N.G.I.   National Gallery of Ireland
N.E.A.C.   New English Art Club
P.R.H.A.   President of the Royal Hibernian Academy
R.A.   Royal Academy
R.D.S.   Royal Dublin Society
R.H.A.   Royal Hibernian Academy

Author's Acknowledgements

Since the preparation of my thesis on Walter Osborne for Trinity College and its subsequent publication as a book in 1974, I have had the opportunity to revise some of my opinions about the artist's work, see new paintings and, most particularly, study more fully the work of his international contemporaries. While, therefore, much of the material contained in this catalogue is based on that in my book, there are, I hope, new insights, which together with the opportunity provided by the Exhibition of seeing the pictures, will lead to a greater appreciation of Osborne's art.

I would like, once again, to express my gratitude to the publishers of my book, Gifford Lewis and Clare Craven, and to all of the people who were so generous with their help when I was working on the book. In addition my thanks are due to my colleagues in the Department of Humanities at Oxford Polytechnic, Andrew Brighton, Clare Tilbury, Keith Wheldon and Jeremy Wood, who read drafts and made useful suggestions; to Julian Campbell, Edward Diestelkamp, Rosamund Fletcher, Peter Howell, Emily Lane; to Dr. Guido Persoons, Librarian of the Royal Academy, Antwerp, and Dr. K. Vanderhoeght, Director of the Stichting Nicolaas Rockox, Antwerp; to the staffs of the National Library of Ireland, the National Gallery of Ireland, the Library of the Victoria and Albert Museum, London; to the owners and custodians of pictures, who have been most generous with their help, and with loans from their collections. In particular my thanks are due to Anne Crookshank, who first suggested Osborne as a topic for research, to Homan Potterton, Director of the National Gallery of Ireland, for making the exhibition possible, and Kim-Mai Mooney of the National Gallery of Ireland, who has organised the exhibition with great patience and efficiency.

Foreword

Exactly eighty years after his death in 1903 and the Memorial Exhibition of his paintings held at the Royal Hibernian Academy in that year, the National Gallery of Ireland is honouring, with a select loan exhibition of his work, one of Ireland's greatest painters: Walter Osborne.

The exhibition is select because it is small, and deliberately so. In contrast to the two hundred and seventy or so pictures exhibited at the Memorial Exhibition, Osborne's lifework is represented in the present exhibition by no more than about one hundred key works including paintings, watercolours and sketches. Like many artists, Osborne's posthumous fortune contrasts markedly with the success he achieved during his lifetime: although his talent was recognised, many of his pictures remained unsold at exhibitions. Today his work is greatly sought after and fetches very high prices. He has been included in major exhibitions of the work of his international contemporaries, and he has been the subject of a modern monograph and *catalogue raisonné* written by Jeanne Sheehy.

The Governors and Guardians of the National Gallery of Ireland were delighted when Jeanne Sheehy kindly accepted their invitation to select and catalogue the present exhibition. She is the expert on Osborne and she is most probably familiar with every brushstroke he painted. In making the Exhibition she has selected those works which represent the artist best and at the different stages of his life. Conscious of his status internationally she has placed his work in an international context by showing in the Exhibition some few works by several of his British, French, Belgian and Dutch contemporaries. By including such items as the sketches with which Osborne annotated exhibition catalogues, she demonstrates the very core of his working methods. Her bibliography on the artist, and the chronology of his life are complete. On behalf of the National Gallery of Ireland it is a pleasure to record a debt of gratitude to Jeanne Sheehy for allowing us to publish the fruits of her researches in this catalogue, and for her willing co-operation in the planning of the Exhibition.

The mounting of any exhibition requires a great deal of organisation. In the case of *Walter Osborne* this has been undertaken with great efficiency by Kim-Mai Mooney, to whom I am most grateful. It is a pleasure also to have the opportunity of placing on record the National Gallery's gratitude to AnCO — the Industrial Training Authority, who, by funding a traineeship in Museum Administration at the National Gallery, have financed Kim-Mai Mooney's work. The catalogue has been typed by Barbara Goff and photography of the exhibits carried out by Declan Emerson and Michael Olohan. The National Gallery's paintings and drawings have been prepared for the Exhibition in our conservation studios by Andrew O'Connor and Maighread McParland, who has been assisted by Pat McBride, Padraic MacGoillarain and David Skinner. Thanks are due to them all. The Exhibition will also be shown in Belfast and the National Gallery is pleased to have the opportunity of collaborating on this occasion with our colleagues in the Ulster Museum.

No loan exhibition is possible without the generosity of those private individuals who are prepared to part with their pictures temporarily so that they may be enjoyed by a wider public. To all lenders to the Exhibition, and in particular to Mrs Sophia Mallin, a relative of the artist who has lent no fewer than five paintings, the Gallery is particularly grateful.

HOMAN POTTERTON
Director, The National Gallery of Ireland

Chronology of Osborne's Life

17th June 1859	Born in Dublin, second son of William Osborne and Anne Jane, née Woods, his wife.
1870	Entered Rathmines School.
1876-81	Pupil in the Schools of the Royal Hibernian Academy, Dublin, and at the Metropolitan School of Art.
14th April 1881	Won Taylor Scholarship (£50) with *A Glade in the Phoenix Park,* at the Royal Dublin Society.
29th Sept. 1881-early in 1883	Pupil at the Académie Royale des Beaux Arts, Antwerp.
19th Oct. 1883	Elected Associate, Royal Hibernian Academy.
Early 1883-early 1884	In Brittany, working at Pont-Aven, Quimperlé and Dinan.
1884	Worked at Lincoln, Southwold and Walberswick.
12th Oct. 1884	Worked at North Littleton, near Evesham, Worcs. with Edward Stott and Nathaniel Hill.
Autumn 1885	At Wherwell, near Andover, Hants., with Edward Stott.
18th October 1886	Elected Member, Royal Hibernian Academy.
8th-24th December 1886	First winter Exhibition, Dublin Art Club, of which Osborne was a founding member.
Summer-Autumn 1888	At Uffington, Berkshire, where he was joined in the autumn by Blandford Fletcher.
1890-91	Worked at Rye and Hastings.
12th July 1892	Violet, the painter's sister married W.F.P. Stockley and went to Canada.
1892	Osborne worked in Dublin and Galway.
18th April 1893	Violet Stockley, née Osborne, died in childbirth.
1893	Bronze Medal for *The Ferry,* World Columbian Exhibition, Chicago. Osborne worked in Limerick and Galway.
December 1895	Travelled in France and Spain with Walter Armstrong.
1896	Travelled in Holland with Walter Armstrong.
1900	Bronze Medal for *Mrs Noel Guinness,* Exposition Internationale, Paris. Declined Knighthood.
24th April 1903	Died, 5 Castlewood Avenue. Buried at Mt. Jerome Cemetary, Dublin.

Introduction

When Walter Osborne died in 1903 a community of British artists got together and bought *An October Morning* for the Guildhall Gallery, City of London, 'as a memorial of the esteem and regard in which the late Walter Osborne was held by them'. The list of artists who contributed to the fund* is very interesting and tells us a lot about Osborne's position among the artists of his day. As a young man he had been part of a group of *plein air* naturalists working in England. Several of these, including Edward Stott, H.H. La Thangue and Stanhope Forbes contributed to the fund. Apart from Forbes there are other members of the Newlyn school, a group of painters who settled in Cornwall and depicted the life of the fishing communities. These include Henry Scott Tuke, A. Chevallier Tayler, Fred Hall and T. C. Gotch. Osborne does not seem to have worked at Newlyn, which is surprising when one considers how many of the Newlyn painters he knew, either as a student at Antwerp or later on. Both John R. Reid and Alfred Parsons were painters whose work he had admired in the London exhibitions of the early eighties, Parsons for his landscapes and Reid for his genre scenes. Osborne was also an admirer of Alma-Tadema, whom he seems to have known since his student days. Tadema, too, had studied at Antwerp, though long before Osborne. Herbert J. Draper is another 'classical' painter on the list, and Edwin Abbey an American whose famous *Richard Duke of Gloucester and the Lady Anne* Osborne had seen at the R.A. in 1896. There are also non-painters, Reginald Blomfield was an architect, and Alfred Drury a sculptor.

Osborne, then, had a firm place among his British contemporaries, though he had virtually ceased painting in England in the early nineties. He still went to London a lot, and visited the exhibitions. He was even beginning to show signs of establishment success

*Their secretary was A. Chevallier Tayler, and the group consisted of:

E. A. Abbey, R.A., Sir Lawrence Alma-Tadema, R.A., O.M., Austin Batchelor, Frank Baxter, Reginald Blomfield, A.R.A., Percy J. Bovill, Robert Brough, A.R.A. (the late), Arnesby Brown, A.R.A., Gerald Chowne, J. Ronald Clive, T. Watt Cope, Herbert J. Draper, Alfred Drury, A.R.A., Joseph Farquharson, A.R.A., Stanhope A. Forbes, R.A., Henry J. Ford, George Gascoyne, R.E., T. C. Gotch, Fred Hall, Herbert Hampton, Everart Hopkins, R. M. Hughes, G. P. Jacomb-Hood, R.O.I., The Hon. Walter J. James, H. H. La Thangue, A.R.A., L. W. Lund, H. L. Morris, L. C. Nightingale, Alfred Parsons, A.R.A., John R. Reid, R.I., R.O.I., Edward Stott, R.A., Arthur Studd, G. Hillyard Swinstead, R.I., R.B.A., F. H. Townsend, H. S. Tuke, A.R.A., Spencer Watson.

—a pastel, *Life in the Streets, Hard Times* was bought by the Chantrey fund in 1892, and his pictures were hung 'on the line' at the Royal Academy. In Ireland, of course, he was an establishment figure, a Royal Hibernian Academician and Dublin's leading portrait painter, who was even offered a knighthood. He was beginning to have a mild success internationally, though only Bronze medals as yet at Chicago in 1893 and Paris in 1900.

Apart from being an establishment figure Walter Osborne was also a very good painter. All of this makes it surprising that he fell into obscurity — completely forgotten in England, though he has always had a steady following in Ireland. The decline in his reputation outside Ireland was partly caused by the fact that he died young, before he had really made his mark, and that early this century *plein air* naturalism was eclipsed by successive waves of enthusiasm for the Parisian avant-garde. Only two pictures of his were in public collections in England, *Life in the Streets, Hard Times* in the Tate, and *Summertime* at Preston, and there were very few in private collections. As a result Osborne had been seen, until recently, solely in the context of Irish painting, isolated from the influences that went into his work — his training at Antwerp, his contacts with French naturalism, his involvement in British *plein air* painting. This catalogue is an attempt to show him in the context of European art in the last third of the nineteenth century, as well as putting together, for the first time since the Memorial Exhibition held at the Royal Hibernian Academy in the winter of 1903-04, a representative selection of Walter Osborne's work.

Osborne's Early Life

Walter Osborne was born on 17th June 1859, the second son of William Osborne, an animal painter who specialised in dogs and horses.[1] Like his more academically brilliant brother, Charles, Walter was sent to Dr. Benson's School at Rathmines, not far from 5 Castlewood Avenue where the Osbornes lived. Walter's school career was respectable, but not distinguished, and he seems to have left when he was sixteen, in the summer of 1875.[2] Since his father was a painter, and a member of the Royal Hibernian Academy (he became an Associate in 1854, and a full member in 1868), there can have been little opposition to Walter's becoming a painter as well. Another artistic connection of the family was Frederic Burton, the watercolour painter who was Director of the National Gallery, London, 1874-1894.[3]

The young Osborne may have spent some time in his father's studio after leaving school, since he did not enter the Schools of the Royal Hibernian Academy until 1876, and he began to do very well almost at once. In his first year he took four out of seven annual prizes:

First prize, a silver medal, for drawing from the living model.
Second prize of £3 for the best collection of meritorious works.
£5 for the greatest number of meritorious works from the Antique.
Second prize of £2 for the best drawing made during the session.

In 1879 he again won a bronze medal for drawing from the antique, a prize of £5, also for drawing from the antique, and a second prize of £3 for the greatest number of meritorious works from the living model. The following year he won £5 for a study in the painting class, and the highest prize the Academy had to offer, the Albert Prize of £20 for *A Glade in the Phoenix Park,* exhibited at the Royal Hibernian Academy in 1880. From all of this it can be seen that not only did he have a very successful student career, but that he followed the conventional art training of the period, moving from the antique to the life class, and eventually graduating to painting in oils.[4] He also seems to have attended classes at the Metropolitan School of Art in Kildare Street, which was associated with the South Kensington system, and came under the Department of Science and Art.[5]

The Taylor Scholarships were inaugurated in 1878 by the Royal Dublin Society. They were awarded for paintings in oils, and the larger prizes were used to send young Irish art students to study abroad. Osborne won their £10 prize in 1879 and in 1800, and in 1881 he won their major prize of £50, Ireland's answer to the *Prix de Rome,* the highest award available to an Irish art student at the time. The judges, who included Sir Thomas Jones P.R.H.A., and Henry Doyle, Director of the National Gallery, recommended that he continue his studies in an English or foreign school of art.[6] Osborne chose the *Académie Royale des Beaux Arts* at Antwerp.

Fig. 1 — *A Life Class in the Antwerp School of Art,* (The Studio, 1893, Vol. I)

Antwerp Years

In the autumn of 1881 Osborne set out for Antwerp, in the company of two fellow Irish painters, J. M. Kavanagh and Nathaniel Hill. In recommending that he continue his studies, it is interesting that the judges of the Taylor Scholarship should have suggested that he might go further afield than England. Earlier in the century London was where Irish painters went to get a bit of polish and make their mark, but by the seventies it was usual for them, like their English contemporaries, to turn to the Continent. Why did Walter Osborne and his friends choose Antwerp?

So much emphasis has been placed on Paris as the centre of all artistic activity in the nineteenth century that people have tended to forget that other places had flourishing artistic communities, academies and schools. Antwerp was one of these. The Royal Academy of Fine Arts, though it had a history going back to the seventeenth century, owed its nineteenth century form to re-organisation in the eighteenth century, and it had a widespread reputation, particularly because of the Belgian school of history painting.[7] Many of the Antwerp history and genre painters were leading figures in European art. Gustave Wappers was Director of the Academy from 1839-45, and he was followed by Nicaise de Keyser between 1855-1879. Henry Leys (1815-69), much honoured and decorated through Europe lived and worked in Antwerp. Charles Verlat, Professor of Paintings 1877-83, and subsequently Director had an international reputation as a painter and as a teacher. The schools drew pupils from all over the world — mainly from Europe, of course, but even from as far afield as Turkey or the United States. There were large numbers from 'Angleterre' (which included, as we shall see, Ireland) in the late seventies, and they increased sharply in the early eighties — 38 in 1881 and 43 in 1882.[8] Two very different members of the English school of painting, Ford Madox Brown and Lawrence Alma-Tadema, had had their early training in the schools of the Antwerp Academy. So it is not really surprising to find so many students there from England and Ireland. In the seventies and eighties it particularly attracted artists who were later to be associated with naturalist painting in England. George Clausen spent a brief period in Antwerp and 'although his acquaintance with the teaching methods of the Antwerp Academy was brief it had a startling effect'.[9] Many of those painters who later settled in Newlyn in Cornwall were also Antwerp trained

> 'Gotch had visited Antwerp and, through Verlat's Academy in that city passed also Harris and Wainwright and Garstin, Bramley and Hall.'[10]

Blandford Fletcher, a friend of Stanhope Forbes who had a brief flirtation with Newlyn, was in Osborne's class at the Academy. William Logsdail, like Bramley and Hall, belonged to a group of painters who went to Antwerp from Lincoln School of Art.[11] From Newcastle came Charles Napier Hemy and his brother Thomas, as well as the aptly named Herbert Schmaltz, though he can scarcely be described as a naturalist.[12] William Spittle, George Winkles and Frederick Davis, contemporaries of Osborne in the life class, all arrived from Birmingham. Antwerp, then, clearly had a reputation among British artists. Both Stanhope Forbes and Norman Garstin, when they spoke of the impulse that had brought the Newlyn group together, coupled the studios of Paris and Antwerp.[13] R. Jope Slade, in an article on "The Outsiders, Some Eminent Artists of the Day Not members of the Royal Academy', published in 1893, wrote that

> 'In five cases out of six the English course is succeeded by a visit to the lapidaries of Paris — Bonnat, Boulanger, Carolus-Duran, Cabanel, Dagnan-Bouveret, Cormon or another; sometimes it is that fine teacher, the late M. Verlat of Antwerp . . .'.[14]

while in the same year Alick Ritchie wrote in *The Studio* that

> 'Britain is, or ought to be, grateful to Antwerp, for it is here that many of her sons, fleeing South Kensington and her system, have studied free of charge from time to time, whose names are now, to borrow an expression from a well-known advertisement, household words in the world of Art. . . . It is not necessary here to give a list of well known English artists who spent a goodly portion of their student days in the schools . . . but the number of those who chose Antwerp in preference to Paris would probably surprise many who think all foreign influence on British art must be French.[15]

It becomes apparent that for many British artists Antwerp was an acceptable alternative to Paris, and that they tended to go there in groups from provincial art schools. Quite apart from whatever artistic reasons there may have been, they may have been sent to Antwerp precisely because it was *not* Paris. Paris had a reputation for wickedness, and parents may have felt that Antwerp offered less distractions to a young man. Also

> 'If not too fond of frequenting music-halls and other places of amusement (presumably, of course, for the purpose of character study) the cost of living will, on the whole, be found cheaper at Antwerp than in most educational centres.'[16]

The first Irish painter to have gone there seems to have been Vincent Gernon, who was there 1877-80.[17] Osborne and his friends were preceded, the previous year, by Norman Garstin, a Limerick born artist who later became a leading member of the Newlyn colony.[18] Either Gernon or Garstin may have been the

16

means by which the younger Dublin artist heard about the school. Osborne registered for the *Natuur* (painting and drawing from life) class on 29th September 1881. He counted among the 'Anglais' — indeed the clerks in charge of admissions clearly had a very hazy idea of the geographical relationship between the two islands, so that we find Peter Keelan in 1878 coming from Irlande (Angleterre), Norman Garstin in 1880 from Limerick (Angleterre) and Osborne in 1881 from Dublin (Angleterre). Foreigners mostly attended the *Natuur* class — foreign students formed a large proportion of the class. Drawing was taught by Polydore Beaufaux, and painting by Charles Verlat.[19] Verlat had been called back to Antwerp in 1877 to become professor of painting under the Directorship of Nicaise de Keyser. The latter retired in 1879, and though Verlat was invited to succeed him he suggested the sculptor Joseph Geefs, who was his senior. In the meantime a Commission was set up to re-organise the Academy, so that when Verlat eventually became Director in 1885 he found himself at the head of 'an academy weakened in its teaching by the suppression of several essential classes' which prevented him from fulfilling 'what might have been expected of him'.[20] During the period of about eighteen months when Osborne was there (he also registered for the Summer course 30th May 1882, and the winter course for a second session 26th September 1882), the academy was in a state of transition. Verlat was clearly an influential teacher, and a factor in the popularity of the Academy — biographies of British artists who studied there nearly always say 'Antwerp under Verlat', rather than just Antwerp.

When they first arrived Osborne, Hill and Kavanagh lodged at 49 Kloosterstraat,[21] not far from where the imposing classical pile of the new Musée Royale des Beaux Arts was under construction.[22] By 1882, while Hill and Kavanagh stayed at Kloosterstraat, Osborne had moved to 12 Keyserstraat,[23] where fellow lodgers were the Birmingham artists William Spittle and Frederick Davis, and Fred Hall from Yorkshire. Keyserstraat was just around the corner from the Academy, and No. 12 was part of the house of the seventeenth century merchant Nicolaas Rockox, friend of Rubens.[24] It seems to have been a popular lodging for art students. We do not, as yet, know much about student life in Antwerp at the time, though Van Gogh's letters[25] suggest that the town was far from dull, and Dermod O'Brien, who went there in the late eighties seems to have worked hard in the studios and had a fairly riotous time otherwise. The day began at 9 o'clock with four hours painting, followed by a meal, then sketching all afternoon until about five, and possibly an evening class later on.[26] There seems to have been a fairly lively international crowd of art students — Blandford Fletcher, who was in the *Natuur* class with Osborne in 1881, remembered his fellow countrymen William Wainwright, Frank Bramley, Fred Hall and William Breakspeare, a Dutchman called de Jongh 'very clever, well known' and Timmermans.[27] The highlight of the year was the *Concours,* in the summer, when the students competed in painting from life. In between courses the students went off on painting expeditions — Osborne worked in Bruges during one of his breaks,[28] and Fletcher went to Brittany in 1881 and 1882. It was to Brittany also that Osborne went early in 1883, after his final course at the Antwerp Academy.

Fig. 2 — *Returning from Labour, Pont-Aven* from Henry Blackburn's 'Breton Folk'

Brittany

Walter Osborne seems to have spent about a year in Brittany, working at Quimperlé, Pont-Aven and Dinan. It is less surprising that he did go to Brittany, than if he had not. It had grown increasingly popular with painters, attracted by its cheapness, by its picturesqueness (local costumes, local customs, local landscape), and, as it attracted more and more of them, by the cosmopolitan gathering of other artists. Pont-Aven was one of their favourite places:

> 'Pont-Aven is a favourite spot for artists, and a *terra incognita* to the majority of travellers in Brittany. Here the art student who has spent the winter in the *Quartier*

Latin in Paris comes when the leaves are green. . . . Pont-Aven has one advantage over other places in Brittany, its inhabitants in their picturesque costume (which remains unaltered) have learned that to sit as a model is a pleasant and lucrative profession and they do this for a small fee without hesitation or *'mauvaise honte'*. This is a point of great importance to the artist. . . .'

wrote Henry Blackburn in 1880, adding that

'a painter might well make Quimperlé a centre of operations, for its precincts are little known, and the gardens shine with laden fruit trees, and the hills are rich in colour until late in Autumn'[29].

Blackburn's impressions are confirmed by the Irish painter Henry Jones Thaddeus[30] who was in Brittany for a while in 1881-82.

'Pont-Aven, not far from Concarneau, is a tranquil sleepy village, with one long street, terminating in the bridge over the Aven; the villagers, in their picturesque Breton costumes, providing the distinctive note so highly prized by painters. When in summer they arrive, laden with canvasses, knapsacks, and easels, local laws and mandates are made to conform to their wishes, and the village is given up to their sweet will. Comprising all nationalities and representing every school of painting, the cosmopolitan crowd devotes itself equally to the spoiling of canvas and to a thorough enjoyment of open-air life. . . .
Nobody came to Pont-Aven in those days excepting painters, and they regarded the place as their own private property. The village itself resembled a gigantic studio, with its picturesque streets full of painters at work, whilst the villagers, from long, practice, were excellent models, and posed anywhere and everywhere'.[31]

Caldecott's illustration *Returning from Labour, Pont-Aven* (fig. 2) depicts not the expected peasant with a hoe or a hayrake, but an artist laden with easel, canvas and painting gear. Osborne may well have stayed at the Pension Gloanec, where lodging was more moderate than at the hotels, the *Lion d'Or* or the *Hotel des Voyageurs*.[32] Given the way Brittany exerted an attraction on so many painters, it is not surprising that Osborne went there, but there were also two fairly strong influences pushing him in that direction. Augustus Burke, who taught Osborne in the Schools of the Royal Hibernian Acadmey[33] had already begun exhibiting Breton scenes in Dublin in the seventies — including *On the Feast of Notre Dame de Trémalo* at the R.H.A. in 1876. Indeed there was quite a strong Breton presence at the R.H.A. in those years. In addition to this Blandford Fletcher had begun to visit Brittany while still a pupil at South Kensington in the late seventies. In the summer of 1881, just before Osborne arrived at Antwerp, Fletcher had been to Brittany, where he met Stanhope Forbes and 'Trifle' Rowe.[34] The following year he was at Pont-Aven again, and at Concarneau, where he met Jules Bastien-Lepage, the French painter who was such a strong influence on young artists at the period. Whistler's friend and disciple Mortimer Menpes was also there. A large number of people associated with naturalist painting in Britain seem to have been in Brittany at this time. George Clausen was painting at Quimperlé in 1882.[35] H. H. La Thangue worked at Cancale with Stanhope Forbes.[36] Though there is no direct evidence, it seems extremely likely that Osborne made contact with some or all of them at this period. His painting in the eighties has a great deal in common with theirs, and he noticed and admired their work at the London exhibitions in 1884 and 1885. It is also significant that there was a remarkable influx of English painters (Fletcher, Forbes, Menpes, Trythall Rowe, Dick Toovey) and Breton subjects at the R.H.A. in 1884, the year that Osborne showed his Breton work. Brittany was clearly a place where Osborne absorbed all kinds of influences, and made contacts and friendships among other artists.

England

After he returned from France in 1883-4 Osborne kept up the habit of working in small rural communities. He would lodge at an inn or cottage in an English village, usually in the company of other painters. 'When I knew him first he used to appear in Dublin towards mid-winter, after sheer cold drove him to shelter like some creature of the fields'. wrote Stephen Gwynn, who first got to know Osborne in about 1884.[37] He was a lifelong friend of Osborne's, and saw a lot of him when he was an undergraduate at Brasenose College, Oxford, 1882-1886, and later a schoolmaster at Bradfield, in Berkshire.[38] From him we get the most complete evocation, apart from the paintings, of Osborne's existence at this time:

> 'living ... in the open air all day, painting from morning to night, and lodging sometimes in a cottage, sometimes in a village inn. He boasted to me once that he had got down his rate of living to twelve shillings a week, though cheapness, he admitted, was the only attraction of that particular lodging, and it was chosen because nothing else offered in the village he had pitched on. But everywhere he lived with extreme frugality, and his way of life kept him in hard training — as strong and active a man as could be found'.[39]

At this period the painter spent the summer and autumn months staying in small villages in Oxfordshire, Berkshire and Hampshire, at Uffington or Newbury, or at Steventon, near Didcot, or North Littleton, near Evesham. When he first returned from Brittany he and Hill worked on the Suffolk coast, at Walberswick, possibly drawn there by Augustus Burke, who had taught them in the schools of the Royal Hibernian Academy. Both Burke and Osborne sent views of Walberswick to exhibitions in 1884.[40] Wilson Steer later remembered meeting both Hill and Osborne there in the eighties.[41] In the autumn of 1884 he was at North Littleton with Hill and an English painter called Edward Stott. Stott (1855-1918) was born in Rochdale, and attended the Manchester School of Art. He studied in Paris under Carolus Duran, and later Cabanel at the *Ecole des Beaux Arts*. He also saw Bastien's *Joan of Arc* at the Salon of 1880, and met the influential young painter.[42] It is not clear where he met Osborne — perhaps Stott, too, was in Brittany in 1883. His work is very close to Osborne's in the mid-eighties, though later they developed different manners based on their early *plein air* interests. Stott suffered from financial hardship in his early life, a fact reflected in one of Osborne's letters home:

> 'I have lent Stott £3 until his people send him some so I am short until he pays me. It is all right, I know, as he is a sterling good fellow and would do nothing dishonourable'.[43]

Another frequent companion at this period was William Teulon Blandford Fletcher (1858-1937). Fletcher had studied at the School of Art in South Kensington before going to Antwerp, where he was in Osborne's class. The two probably also visited Brittany together. Fletcher, too, painted rural *plein air* subjects, though, unlike Osborne, his manner did not alter greatly throughout his career. He was briefly associated with the community of naturalist painters who settled at Newlyn, in Cornwall, and was a friend of Stanhope Forbes. Given his association with so many of the Newlyn painters, it is odd that Osborne does not seem to have gone there at all. Osborne and Fletcher worked together at Newbury in 1887, and at Uffington during the autumn of 1888 — on 23rd November Osborne did a small drawing of Fletcher seated in an armchair smoking a pipe.[44] The two men also worked together at Rye and at Steventon. At this same period Osborne was an enthusiastic visitor to the London galleries, especially the more avant-garde ones such as the Grosvenor Gallery. He was also involved with the New English Art Club from the second, more solid, year of its existence. The club was founded because of:

> 'a fresh wave of foreign influence in the person of a number of students who had worked in Parisian Schools ... most of them, to become known as the Newlyn school, had found their inspiration in the *plein air* painting of Bastien Lepage'.[45]

and also

> 'with a view to protesting against the narrowness of the Royal Academy and to obtaining fuller recognition for the work of English artists who had studied in France'.[46]

The founding members included many of Osborne's friends and painting companions — Wilson Steer, Trythall Rowe, Edward Stott, and fellow students from Antwerp like Fred Hall and

William Logsdail. Walter Osborne began to exhibit with them in 1887, and is listed as a member from 1889. His first exhibit at the New English was *October by the Sea* probably the painting eventually presented to the Guildhall in his memory, (Cat. No. 18), and many of the contributors to the memorial had been closely involved with the Club. In 1889 and 1890 Osborne is listed as a member of the New English, but does not seem to have shown any pictures — can it possibly be that his work was rejected? After that he ceased to be a member for several years — perhaps he was eclipsed with other *plein air* painters when the Club was dominated by a group of English Impressionists led by Steer, Sickert and Fred Brown. He re-appeared in 1899, when his work had taken him closer to the Paris influenced English Impressionists, away from the *plein air* interests of his youth. By this time the New English could be described thus by George Moore:

> 'The New English Art Club is very typical of this end of the century. It is young, it is interesting, it is intelligent, it is emotional, it is cosmopolitan — not the Bouillon Duval cosmopolitanism of the Newlyn School, but rather an agreeable assimilation of the Montmartre café of fifteen years ago'.[47]

Osborne clearly gave careful attention to the commercial aspects of his profession — the exhibition and sale of his pictures. There is some indication of this in one of his early letters home to his father:

> 'I think I forgot to tell you that I received a letter from Nottingham in answer to mine referring them to Mrs (?) Brown. . . . I wrote back however and told them that I had other work in Liverpool that I would be happy to submit and asking them for particulars of their intended exhibition etc. The annual ex is a good selling place I believe'.[48]

A glance at the catalogue entries will show how he moved his paintings around, and sometimes, if they did not sell, he would even lower the price. He exhibited regularly, of course, in Dublin — especially at the Royal Hibernian Academy, to which he sent his first exhibit in 1877. He also began to exhibit at Liverpool while he was still a student — in 1882 he sent *The Tempting Bait,* the picture with which he had won the Taylor Scholarship for the second time.

His connection with Liverpool is not surprising — his father had been exhibiting there since 1873, and there was a special relationship between the R.H.A. and the Walker Art Gallery. In 1884 the Walker had a room devoted to work from the R.H.A. The only other English provincial gallery to which Walter Osborne sent pictures regularly was the Royal Birmingham Society of Artists, where he exhibited throughout his life. Perhaps he was drawn there because of the contacts he had made with several Birmingham artists at Antwerp. Otherwise he exhibited at the London galleries. One of these, as we have seen, was the New English Art Club. He also exhibited with the Institute of Painters in Oil Colours (from 1894 known as the Society of Oil Painters) from their second exhibition in 1884, and he was a member from 1891. He was a regular in the annual exhibitions of the Royal Academy, beginning in 1886 with *Tired Out,* though he mainly sent portraits in the later part of his career. In 1892 a pastel of his *Life in the Streets, Hard Times,* was bought for 25 guineas under the terms of the Chantrey Bequest. The sculptor, Sir Francis Chantrey had left a sum of money, the interest from which was to be used to purchase British art for the nation, and the first purchase was made in 1877.[49] Being the subject of a Chantrey purchase was considered an establishment honour, and is perhaps an indication that Osborne was beginning to attain general recognition, though it is a pity that they did not choose a better picture. By the time the purchase was made, in 1892, Osborne had already begun to change the pattern of his working life, and had deserted the English villages to work more in Ireland.

Fig. 3 — *Walter Osborne in his Studio in St. Stephen's Green*

The Later Years in Ireland

During his student days, and even while he was still doing a great deal of his painting in England, Osborne remained an active member of Dublin's artistic community. He was elected Associate of the Royal Hibernian Academy in 1883, and a full Member in 1886,[50] and he exhibited with the Academy, without missing a year, from 1877 until his death. He taught in the Academy Schools from the early nineties until the end of his life, and was an influential teacher. W. J. Leech said that Osborne had taught him 'everything I needed to know'.[51] He inspired such devotion in Beatrice Elvery's sister, another of his students, that she travelled on the top of a tram in the rain so that she, like Osborne, might catch pneumonia and die.[52] He also took an active part in the life of the Academy, serving on committees, joining deputations to the Lord Lieutenant, acting on committees of enquiry, and helping in the organisation of the winter exhibitions which the Academy began to hold in the nineties.[53]

In 1884 he became a member of the Dublin Sketching Club, founded in 1874 'for the purpose of bringing together artists, amateurs and gentlemen interested in art in friendly and social intercourse'.[54] The club was quite progressive for a time, and in 1884 held a loan exhibition of paintings by Whistler which set Dublin by the ears. 'The whole of Dublin was convulsed and many went to Molesworth to see the exhibition who rarely went to see anything of the kind'.[55] Osborne did not remain a member for very long, but in 1886 we find him among the founding members of the Dublin Art Club, which has all the appearance of being the local equivalent of the New English, founded in the same year. It held its first winter exhibition 8th-24th December 1886, with Osborne on the organising committee. As well as paintings by the members it showed a collection of drawings by Burne-Jones. Conspicuous among the exhibitors at the Dublin Art Club were several of Osborne's companions from Antwerp, Brittany and English *plein air* circles — Edward Stott, T. Trythall Rowe, C. Napier Hemy. Clausen's *Ploughing* was exhibited in 1890, along with three of his pastels. Osborne lent a picture by Fred Hall the same year. We find Fred Brown, Alma-Tadema, Trythall Rowe and Wilson Steer exhibiting the following year, and Francis Bate, author of *The Naturalistic School of Painting,* for many years secretary of the New English, and a fellow pupil of Osborne's from Antwerp, the year after that.[56] All of this suggests that Walter Osborne had an active role in the introduction to Dublin of influences from European and British *plein air* painting. The club probably also played an important part in introducing painters to potential patrons, since it included a category of 'Non-working members' which is full of solid merchant names like Findlater, Jameson, Malcomson, Pim, Todd and Walpole.[57]

Osborne ceased to make painting trips to England in about 1892, and worked instead in the Dublin streets, and in the villages of north County Dublin, with occasional forays elsewhere. He lived with his family at 5 Castlewood Avenue, Rathmines, and from 1895 had a large studio at 7 St Stephen's Green.[58] Stephen Gwynn has suggested that it was devotion to his family that brought him home. In 1892 Walter's sister Violet married and emigrated with her husband, W.F.P. Stockley, to Canada, leaving the parents on their own, since Charles, his elder brother, was a clergyman living in England.[59] Within a year Violet Osborne had died in childbirth, and her daughter, also named Violet, was brought home to be looked after by the Osborne grandparents in Castlewood Avenue. William Osborne had been doing less well with his sporting pictures 'the landlord class who gave him commissions to paint their terriers and hounds and hunters were hard hit by the land war of the 'eighties, and had to retrench in all directions'.[60] In the early nineties Walter Osborne found himself with an aged father, a mother going blind, and a small child on his hands. Gwynn's argument is that these circumstances not only tied him to Ireland, but turned him from landscape to portraiture in order to make enough money.

> 'Walter Osborne, like many Irishmen, was impenetrably reticent about the matters that concerned him most dearly ... and he never talked of such things; but undoubtedly he felt the need to earn more, and portraiture was the obvious resource'.[61]

It is certainly true that the number of portraits he exhibited increased dramatically in the nineties. The character of his painting began to change too. He was subject to new influences, and no longer in close touch with the *plein air* companions of his youth, whose own painting, in any case, was moving in different directions. The change of location affected his painting visually, of course, but also emotionally.

Not that he cut himself off from England and the Continent. He still attended the London exhibitions regularly, as well as exhibiting there, and at Liverpool and Birmingham. In 1895 he made a trip to Spain in the company of Walter Armstrong, who had become Director of the National Gallery of Ireland in 1892. The two men began their journey in Paris, where they 'went everywhere and did everything that respectable citizens ought to do'.[62] Osborne wrote from Bordeaux to Sarah Purser, giving the impression that the visit to Paris was his first. This is interesting, since many people assumed that he had trained in Paris, whereas it seems that he did not even go there while he was working in

Brittany.[63] He visited the Luxembourg, which was at that time the gallery of modern art, but was not much impressed;

> 'I thought if you took away Cazin's study of Gambetta's room, pictures by Friant, Besnard and Manet, there was little left to go wild about and certainly the great mass of the pictures seemed to me leathery in the extreme'.

The Louvre was a different matter:

> 'After seing the Luxembourg I went and spent a day in the Louvre and was enchanted beyond measure with the Rembrandts, Velasquezs, Titians, Leonardo da Vincis, and the wonderful frescoes by Botticelli, also the Holbeins, Metsus, Hals, Van Eycks. Their art is superb, one feels almost speechless in their presence'.[64]

In Spain they visited Madrid and Toledo, and no doubt looked at a great deal of Spanish painting, on which Armstrong was an expert, and in which Osborne became increasingly interested.[65] In 1896 Armstrong and Osborne made a trip together to Holland, and Osborne painted canal scenes in Amsterdam.[66]

Dublin itself was by no means culturally isolated during the nineties, and had plenty of congenial company to offer an artist. George Moore, with his intimate knowledge of the Paris of Manet and Degas, settled for a time in Dublin, and Osborne often visited his house in Ely Place.[67] Hugh Lane was already involved in the activities which led to his setting up the gallery of Modern Art. Lane acquired several paintings by Osborne for the gallery, and regarded him as one of Ireland's few men of genius,[68] though their relations must have been strained when Osborne publicly resigned from the committee of Lane's Winter Exhibition of Old Masters in 1902 because he was doubtful about the attribution of one of the pictures.[69] Osborne's friend Armstrong was also a critic and art historian with a reputation that was not confined to Ireland, and he seems to have done a lot to widen his friend's artistic experience. Bodkin has said[70] that his friends 'were by no means all artists or art lovers, for he had no inveterate taste for such company' yet Osborne does seem to have counted a considerable number of artists among his friends. He was related to Sarah Purser, with whom he corresponded, and who jumped to his defence on at least one occasion. He visited Nathaniel Hone at

Malahide as he worked increasingly in north County Dublin. He kept up with his friends of Antwerp days, especially Nathaniel Hill. He was a friend of John Hughes, and one of the last portraits he did was a watercolour of Hughes, working on his sculpture *Orpheus and Eurydice* (Cat. No. 97). He was friendly with both of the Orpen brothers, William the painter and Richard the architect — he very nearly married their sister Grace.[71] Dermod O'Brien was another close friend — Osborne was best man at his wedding in 1902. Dermod's sister Nellie was another of those women with whom Osborne's name was linked. Another was Betty Webb, who was secretary to Sir Thornley Stoker. The Stokers lived in Ely Place, and Osborne visited them a great deal.[72] His family obligations, and perhaps his comparative lack of money, seem to have prevented Osborne from marrying.[73]

Nobody who wrote or spoke about Walter Osborne expressed anything but liking. Bodkin wrote:[74]

'As he had always shown a generous temperament, a sense of fun and a spirit of sportsmanship, he left a wide circle of personal friends to whom his charming personality had endeared him'.

and Stephen Gwynn remembered him as a convivial man:

'He liked company, he liked games, he liked a good dinner as well as anyone, and he liked the sense that he could drink as much and smoke as much as the most convivial and be not one hair the worse next morning when other heads were sore'.[75]

Even the astringent Susan Mitchell called him:

'Another attractive personality . . . a most competent craftsman, and lovable man'.[76]

He was, Stephen Gwynn tells us, 'studiously normal' in his appearance.

'He was part of the group in which Yeats first became known, and he was somewhat inclined to complain because Yeats not only was a poet, but looked a poet. He, for his part was studiously normal. Neatness, indeed, was part of his general dexterity, and his tall, broad-shouldered figure made matters very easy for his tailor.[77]

Beatrice Elvery[78] said he dressed more like a doctor or a lawyer than a painter. On occasion the artist in him broke out, according to Stephen Gwynn:

> 'I have seen him hanging up his ties out of doors to get the colour weathered; and in his out-door life he always wore some kind of picturesque soft hat, though never on any account in Dublin or in London'.[79]

By 1903 Walter Osborne was a much respected and loved public figure in Dublin society, an Irish artist who 'with a great and growing reputation in England elected to live and work in his own country'.[80] In 1900 he was offered a Knighthood 'in recognition of his services to art and his distinction as a painter,'[81] but he refused. He was Ireland's leading portrait painter, and his portrait of *Mrs Noel Guinness and her Daughter* (Cat. No. 90) had been awarded a bronze medal at the Paris International Exhibition of 1900.[82] He was at the height of his powers as a painter, and probably on the threshold of yet finer artistic achievements. It was a great tragedy, and a shock to all who knew him, when he died suddenly of pneumonia on 23rd April 1903, at the age of forty-three.

Cat. No. 5 — *Beneath St. Jacques, Antwerp*

Cat. No. 7 — *Apple Gathering, Quimperlé*

34

Cat. No. 19 — *Feeding Chickens*

Cat. No. 37 — *Cherry Ripe*

Cat. No. 59 — *Marsh's Library*

Cat. No. 76 — *In the Garden, Castlewood Avenue*

Cat. No. 87 — *Master Aubrey Gwynn*

Cat. No. 88 — *Mrs Andrew Jameson and her daughter Violet*

Early Work: Antwerp & Brittany

Fig. 4 — *Le Coup de Collier* by Charles Verlat, Karel Verlat-Zaal, Antwerp.

Early Work: Antwerp & Brittany

From the beginning Osborne's paintings follow a consistent pattern of preference for landscape and genre, with an interest in animal painting which diminished towards the end of his career. At the age of thirteen he was already talking, in a letter home from Co. Wicklow, of "drawings ... of cows and sheep".[1] Animal paintings also figure largely in his early exhibited works — he was already showing at the Royal Hibernian Academy at the age of eighteen. It seems clear that his father was a powerful influence on his work, though more in choice of subject than in handling. Even at an early age Walter Osborne's paintings are more adventurous in brushwork and more varied in palette than those of his father. This taste for animal painting will have been strengthened at Antwerp where the Professor of Painting, Charles Verlat was renowned as a painter of animals — to the extent that his major works are now housed in a special room at Antwerp Zoo. Apart from the animals it is difficult, at first, to see the connection between Verlat's work and that of pupils like Osborne. His canvases are huge, thickly encrusted with paint, and depict some highly tense moment of dramatic action, with animals as the main actors. *Le Coup de Collier* (fig. 4) shows two carthorses, whipped on by their waggoners, making the ultimate effort to breast a hill above Paris. It was exhibited at the Paris Salon of 1857.[2] There is a kind of loudness and vulgarity about the picture which one associates with Courbet, and very far from the gentlemanly sensibility that is characteristic of nearly all of Osborne's work. It does, however, show qualities of drawing, of application of paint, and of palette, which could have been influential. The colour is varied, and fairly bright, and the brushwork vigorous. Verlat said of it, however 'I am concentrating more on the *drawing* than on the colour',[3] and deprecated what he felt was a neglect of drawing for the sake of colour in Courbet's work. Osborne, too, was thorough in his draughtsmanship, and usually made careful pencil studies for his paintings. On the other hand Verlat is also recorded as saying

> 'It is a great gift for a painter to keep, in his finished work, the spontaneous sensation felt by the eye in front of nature.'[4]

The 'spontaneous sensation' is present in Osborne's work in paintings like *Moderke Verhoft* (Cat. No. 1) and *Market Stall* (Cat. No. 3), small studies where the brushwork is vigorous and at the same time effectively descriptive, and the colour, even when it is limited in palette or low in key, is lively. There was clearly some emphasis on landscape, genre and *plein air* painting in the teaching of the Academy when Osborne was there — landscape classes attracted small numbers which increased sharply around 1880. In 1883 there was a class called *Landscape and Animal Painting.*[5] When Verlat took up his post as Professor in 1877, he was just back from Palestine, which he described as 'a vast studio *en plein air*', and where the light and colour had had a great deal of influence on his work.[6] Dermod O' Brien's painting of the life class in 1890 (Cat. No. 12) is extremely interesting in that the model, a robust working woman with a tired child leaning against her knee, is just the kind of group that we find in French naturalist work, and in pictures of the Hague School. The impression one gets from Van Gogh's studies at the Antwerp Academy is of an old-fashioned, authoritarian institution, hung up on the Belgian history painting of Leys and Wappers, with very little that was inspiring in its teaching.[7] This is difficult to reconcile with the fact that, certainly among the British and Irish, it turned out so many adherents of *plein air* naturalism. It may be that in the reaction against academicism people belittled the influence of the Academy's teaching, or it may be that the influence came from elsewhere. Norman Garstin, the Limerick born painter who became a member of the Newlyn group, is an interesting case:

> 'During his last six months in Belgium, apparently dissatisfied with Verlat as a teacher, he passed his time painting in the countryside with Theodore Verstraete'.[8]

Is Verstraete perhaps the *éminence grise* of the Antwerp School? Verstraete was dedicated to painting from the motif — he built himself a caravan so that he could live near whatever subject that interested him, and installed large windows in it so that he could paint whatever the weather. He painted rather dreamy pictures of peasants in the landscape which have one important characteristic in common with Osborne:

> 'Verstraete saw man in nature as he is, the right size, in proportion to the things that surround him, neither too large nor too small. And he did not separate him from the rest. He did not put him there, he found him there.'[9]

One of the places Verstraete worked was Calmphout, near Antwerp, where Osborne painted *Moderke Verhoft* (Cat. No. 1). It is significant also that Verstraete exhibited at the R.H.A. in 1883.

Osborne's paintings of the Antwerp period, and later, have quite a lot in common with the Hague School, at the height of its reputation the decade before he reached Belgium.[10] *Moderke Verhoft* (Cat. No. 1), for example recalls the peasant interiors of Jozef Israëls (Cat. No. 13), and the fine drawing and delicate detail of *Boy Blowing Bubbles* (Cat. No. 6) is not unlike the sensitive studies of children of Jacob Maris (see Cat. No. 14). His rural themes, and the restricted palette of his early work bring him close to Anton Mauve (see Cat. No. 15). Osborne had in common with the Hague painters what separates them from the French Realists

> 'In contrast to France the focus in the Netherlands was on the depiction not of man, but of the landscape. Only Israëls's position is to some extent comparable. . . . What is lacking, however, is the fierceness, the commitment

that the French brought to their portrayal of the life of the lower classes.... In the work of the Dutch genre painters one does not find any close involvement with the fate of the victims of a harsh social system.'[11]

What is more difficult to establish is how Osborne came into contact with the painters of the Hague School. The relationship between Dutch and Belgian painting at this period has yet to be explored, but many contacts are recorded between Belgian and The Hague painters, and, geographically, The Hague is not very far from Antwerp.[12] It may simply be that similar influences — especially Dutch seventeenth century painting and French Realism — were at work in the two countries.[13] Verlat had a great admiration for the work of Theodore Rousseau and Camille Corot.[14]

Yet another continental influence came into play when Osborne went to Brittany early in 1883, though it may well have been in the air before that. This was the influence of the French naturalist painter Jules Bastien-Lepage (1848-84).

> In every country the most promising youths were frankly imitating his work, with its ideals of exact representation of nature as seen out of doors, everything being painted on the spot in a grey light, in order that there might be as little change in the effect as possible while the artist was at work.[15]

One of the hallmarks of Bastien's work at the height of his fame was what A.S. Hartrick calls the 'square-brush act'.[16] Here is how an English critic described it in 1893:

> 'the ordinary every-day artist, if he wants to paint a ship's mast against the sky, takes a brush coming to a fine point, and draws it vertically up and down his canvas in the place desired. The Newlyner does nothing of the sort. He uses a squarer brush and gets his mast by a series of horizontal strokes...'.[17]

Although Osborne sometimes used the 'square brush', and painted pictures made up of large, interlocking brushstrokes, he did not go overboard for the method. A comparison of *Apple Gathering, Quimperlé* (Cat. No. 7) with a similar painting done

Fig. 5 — *A Breton Girl* by George Clausen,
     Victoria & Albert Museum

by Clausen (fig. 5) the previous year will make this clear. Clausen
uses thick impasto, and brushstrokes which are very consciously

marks on a flat canvas, so that a tension is set up between the depiction of the subject and the medium and support. Osborne occasionally uses this technique, but more subtly, and he generally uses his brushstrokes to model the form. In *Apple Gathering,* though there is some evidence of the 'square brush' — in the painting of the tree, for example — the brushstrokes are on the whole varied according to the character of the object. Another characteristic of Bastien's work which we find in Osborne is the *plein air* subject — usually peasants in a landscape — painted in an even light so that there is a predominance of silvery greens.

He also adopted the other major mark of Bastien and his English followers, the square signature, conspicuously inscribed on the picture. Bastien-Lepage, who died at the age of thirty-six in 1884, was at Concarneau, in Brittany, in 1883,[18] and it is possible that Osborne met him. Osborne's classmate, Blandford Fletcher, had met him at Pont-Aven in 1882,[19] and there is a possibility that Osborne, too, was at Pont-Aven in 1882, during the break between the summer course and the winter course at the Academy.

1 Moderke Verhoft
c.1882

Oil on panel, 21.1 x 13.3 cm. (8 x 5⅞ ins.)

Inscribed, verso: *A Study. Moderke Verhoft van Calmphout; Mother Verhoft from Calmphout, near Antwerp, by* **Walter Osborne**[20]

PROVENANCE: Sherlock Bequest, 1941. N.G.I. Cat. No. 1929

EXHIBITED: *Irish Art in the 19th Century,* Crawford Art Gallery, Cork, 1971, (111).

LITERATURE: Sheehy, (1974), no. 25.

It is significant that this is described as 'A Study'. It has a freedom and confidence that Osborne did not always achieve in his more finished work early in his career. The colour is superb — lit up by vivid touches which are, at the same time, integrated into the overall harmony. The subject has affinities with the French Realist tradition, and with the Hague painters. The resemblance to early work by Van Gogh (*The Potato Eaters,* Van Gogh Museum, Amsterdam) is a reminder that he, too, had connections with the Hague School, and studied for a short time at Antwerp.

Lent by the National Gallery of Ireland

2   The Flemish Cap
1882

Etching, 21.5 x 15.2 cm. (8½ x 6 ins.)

Signed and dated, top left: **F. W. Osborne 1882.**

LITERATURE: Sheehy, (1974), no. 34.

Verlat was a keen etcher, and Osborne made this etching, and another of a dog, while a student at the Academy. It was not a medium in which he persisted, or which suited him very well. The signature is the one Osborne used in his earliest work, before he adopted the square capitals of the *plein air* school.

Lent by Professor Aloys Fleischmann

3　A Market Stall *1882*

Oil on canvas, 29.2 x 34.3 cm. (11½ x 13½ ins.)

Signed and dated, bottom left: **F. Walter Osborne 1882.**

LITERATURE: Sheehy, (1974), no. 24.

A marvellously fresh picture in which the sunlight, filtering through the trees, lights up, in vivid slashes of green, the vegetables on the stall. The date suggests that this picture was painted in Belgium, and it is a study for 'another picture with figures in Flemish costume. Perhaps one of them is *In the Market Place of Bruges,* exhibited at the R.H.A. in 1884. Osborne is still using the early form of his name, F. Walter Osborne, though he has adopted the square capitals of Bastien-Lepage. There is some suggestion, too, of the 'square brush' — in the tree trunk, for example. Is this an indication that Bastien's influence was already pervasive in Antwerp, or did Osborne go to Brittany in the summer of 1882?

Private Collection

4 View in Antwerp
1881-82

Oil on board, 21.6 x 12.7 cm. (8½ x 5 ins.)

Signed, bottom right: **F.W.O.,** and bottom left; **F. W. Osborne**

LITERATURE: Sheehy, (1974), no. 29.

This is a painting from Osborne's student days, possibly painted during his first session at the Academy. The site is not far from his first lodgings in Kloosterstraat. The tower is that of the Church of St. Charles Borromeo, originally the Jesuit Church of St. Ignatius. The picture is possibly *Antwerp from a Bend of the Scheldt* exhibited at the R.H.A. in 1883.

Private Collection

51

5 Beneath St. Jacques, Antwerp

Oil on canvas, 66 x 45.7 cm. (26 x 18 ins.)

Signed and dated, bottom left: **F. W. Osborne 82.**

PROVENANCE: Formerly collection of Paul Curran

EXHIBITED: R.H.A., 1883, (48), £30.

LITERATURE: Sheehy, (1974), no. 26; *Irish Times*, 8/7/78.

This is painted in the narrow range of greys and beiges characteristic of much of Osborne's early work, and the figures are rather wooden and tentatively drawn. However, there is some very sensitive observation, what the painter would probably have called 'truth', in the sunlight falling through the doorway and on the wall of the house. St. Jacques was just round the corner from where Osborne had his lodgings in 1882.

Private Collection

6 Boy Blowing Bubbles

Oil on canvas, 31 x 23 cm. (12 x 9 ins.)

Signed bottom left: **Walter Osborne**

PROVENANCE: Sherlock Bequest, 1949.
N.G.I. Cat. No. 1053.

LITERATURE: Sheehy, (1974), no. 6.

It has not been possible to date this
picture with any precision. It has
affinities with Dutch genre painting,
especially with Jacob Maris (Cat. No.
14).

Lent by the National Gallery of Ireland

7 Apple Gathering, Quimperlé *1883*

Oil on canvas, 58 x 46 cm. (22¼ x 17¼ ins.)

Signed and dated, bottom left: **Walter Osborne Quimperlé 1883**

PROVENANCE: Sherlock Bequest, 1940. N.G.I. Cat. No. 1052.

EXHIBITED: R.H.A., 1884, (90), 30 gns; *Autumn Exhibition,* Walker Art Gallery, Liverpool, 1884, (888), 30 gns; *Ierse Schilders der 19ᵉ en 20ᵉ eeuw,* Stedelijk Museum Amsterdam, 1951, (30); *Post Impressionism,* R.A., 1979-80, (326); *The Peasant in French 19th Century Art,* The Douglas Hyde Gallery, Dublin, 1980, (81).

LITERATURE: Sheehy, (1974), no. 61; Exhibition catalogues (see above); Post Impressionism, p. 203; *The Peasant in French 19th Century Art,* p. 190.

The square signature and the indication of location are characteristic of Bastien's work, as are the grey-green palette and the rural subject matter. There is a suggestion of the 'square brush' in his handling, but on the whole it is varied to suit the modelling of the object depicted. The colour is treated with great sureness, even panache — notice the almost gratuitous touch of pink above the stooping figure — though the figure drawing is rather wooden.

Lent by the National Gallery of Ireland

8 View of a Town

c.1883

Oil on board, 21 x 12.7 cm. (8½ x 5 ins.)

Signed, bottom left: **F. W. Osborne**

PROVENANCE: Miss Violet Stockley, to the present owner by descent.

LITERATURE: Sheehy, (1974), no. 87.

This may be Brittany — the church tower looks like that of Quimperlé, and the turret on the right looks French, but it is difficult to be certain. It has more than a suggestion of the 'square brush', and the free handling and subtle colour characteristic of the period.

Lent by Mrs Sophia Mallin

a   b   c

Three Pencil Sketches, by WALTER OSBORNE, R.H.A., b.1859 ; d.1903

9 Three Pencil Sketches *1882-84?*

Pencil on white paper, a: 6.5 x 8.5 cm. (2½ x 3⅜ ins.); b: 8.2 x 6.5 cm. (3¼ x 2½ ins.); c: 6.5 x 5 cm. (2½ x 2 ins.)

PROVENANCE: Presented by Miss Jane French through the Friends of the National Collections, 1939. N.G.I. Cat. Nos. 2976, 6266, 6267.

LITERATURE: Sheehy, (1974), no. 33.

These are probably pages from a sketchbook — perhaps one kept by Osborne while he was a student abroad, and in his early days in England. The costumes of the seated man and the woman sewing suggest Holland or Belgium. The standing, agricultural figures of the man and woman could be English.

Lent by the National Gallery of Ireland

56

10 Landscape *1883*

Oil on board, 31.1 x 21 cm. (12¼ x 8¼ ins.)

Signed and dated, bottom left: **F. W. Osborne 83.**

PROVENANCE: Canon C. E. Osborne bequest, 1971.

LITERATURE: Sheehy, (1974), no. 64.

The date suggests that this was painted in Brittany, though there is little in the subject to attach it to a particular location. It is the kind of simple, unemphatic landscape we find throughout Osborne's career — he does not seem to have been drawn to the kind of spectacular romantic landscape in which his own country is so abundant.

Lent by The Hugh Lane Municipal Gallery of Modern Art, Dublin

WALTER OSBORNE.

11 Landscape *c.1883*

Oil on board, 21 x 12.7 cm. (8¼ x 5 ins.)

Signed, bottom left: **Walter Osborne**

PROVENANCE: Canon C. E. Osborne bequest, 1971.

LITERATURE: Sheehy, (1974), no. 160.

It has the delicacy of colour and sureness of touch characteristic of his landscape studies of this period. The architecture suggests France.

Lent by The Hugh Lane Municipal Gallery of Modern Art, Dublin

12   Dermod O'Brien
(1865-1945)

The Fine Art Academy,
Antwerp *1890*

Oil on canvas, 80 x 58.5 cm. (31½ x 23 ins.)

Signed and dated: **D. O'Brien -90.**

PROVENANCE: Pyms Gallery, London, where purchased, 1982.

EXHIBITED: *The Irish Revival,* Pyms Gallery, London, 1982, (5).

This was painted when O'Brien was a pupil at Antwerp. O'Brien and Osborne became close friends, though they were not students together. What is interesting about this painting of the life class is that the group is the kind of genre group one associates with naturalist painting. It is not unlike some of Osborne's Dublin pictures of the nineties.

Lent by The Ulster Museum, Belfast

13   Jozef Israëls *(1824-1911)*

Old Man with a Child in a High Chair

Oil on panel, 29 x 39 cm. (11½ x 15¼ ins.)

Signed: **Jozef Israels**

PROVENANCE: Sir Alfred Chester Beatty
Gift, 1950. N.G.I. Cat. No. 4242 CB.

Jozef Israëls was a painter of the
Hague School, whose work has quite a
lot in common with many of the
Antwerp Academy pupils. There is no
evidence that Osborne knew Israëls,
but he probably came into contact with
his work, especially as it was popular in
England.[21] The handling, and the
concentration on *chiaroscuro* in this
picture are very different from
Osborne's work, but the subject matter
— peasant subject and dark interior
—is one that occurs in Osborne — see,
for example, *Moderke Verhoft* (Cat.
No. 1) or *A Galway Cottage* (Cat. No.
63). Osborne, like Israëls, was fond of
painting children.

Lent by the National Gallery of Ireland

14 Jacob Maris
(1837-99)

A Girl Feeding a Bird in a Cage

Oil on panel, 32.6 x 20.8 cm. (12⅞ x 8¼ ins.)

Signed, bottom right: **J Maris f.**

PROVENANCE: (Given in full in Maclaren, see Literature, below). Acquired c.1905 by Sir Hugh Lane; Lane Bequest, 1917. Cat. No. 3261.

EXHIBITED: Grafton Galleries, London, 1896, (124); Goupil Gallery, London, 1898, (20); Preston, 1902, (45); Guildhall, London, 1903, (31); R.H.A., 1904-05, (125); National Museum, Dublin, 1905, (78).

LITERATURE: N. Maclaren, *National Gallery Catalogues, The Dutch School,* (London, 1960), p. 236.

Jacob Maris was another Hague School painter, and studied at the Antwerp Academy around 1854, where he was a fellow pupil of Alma-Tadema.[22] There are qualities in the precision of his drawing, and in the subtlety of his palette, which are reminiscent of early Osborne. Maris could be very painterly in approach, as in the background of this picture, and the subject too has affinities with Osborne.

Lent by the Trustees of the National Gallery, London

15　Anton Mauve *(1838-88)*

A Shepherd and Sheep

Oil on panel, 33 x 41 cm. (13 x 16⅛ ins.)

Signed: **A. Mauve**

PROVENANCE: Sir Alfred Chester Beatty Gift, 1950. N.G.I. Cat. No. 4257 CB.

Anton Mauve was also a leading member of the Hague School. His rural subject matter, with figures and animals, has a lot in common with Osborne's early *plein air* work — see for example *A Shepherd and his Flock* (Cat. No. 26). His palette, with its restricted range of blues, beiges and greens, is very close to some of Osborne's paintings of the eighties, and so, too, is his combination of precise drawing and painterly handling.

Lent by the National Gallery of Ireland

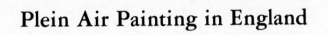

Plein Air Painting in England

Fig. 6 — *Ploughing* by George Clausen, Aberdeen Art Gallery and Museums.

Plein Air Painting in England

Osborne's paintings of the eighties continue along similar lines to his work in Antwerp and Brittany — rural genre scenes, and occasionally pure landscape. More often than not his figures are just part of the countryside, generalised types rather than individuals. In this he differs from Bastien-Lepage, who was such an influence on the British naturalists[1] and from English contemporaries like Clausen — compare, for example Osborne's *Ploughing* (Cat. No. 32) with Clausen's (fig. 6). He painted peasants in the landscape not out of social or political conviction, but because the kind of painting that interested him belonged to the French Realist tradition which had had strong social and political overtones. In his youth he was attracted by the notion of painting directly from the motif, and of 'truth' to nature (see section on his annotated catalogues), and, because of the circumstances of his training in Antwerp and Brittany, these qualities came associated with pictures of peasant and seafaring life.

He also differed from many naturalists in not being attached to a particular place. Bastien-Lepage had said:

> 'I come from a village in Lorraine. I mean, first of all, to paint the peasants and landscapes of my home exactly as they are.'[2]

Edward Stott eventually settled at Amberley in Sussex, and the Newlyners devoted themselves to the life and landscape of the Cornish coast. Osborne had no such attachments and Stephen Gwynn recalled that:

> 'Dublin-bred, he was only a countryman by choice of his adult life: and although he knew the detail of English (not Irish) country life more intimately perhaps than any one with whom I have been acquainted, yet he had not on him the stamp of those who have passed their childhood in the country.... Osborne loved the country with a feeling that pervades all his studies of its beauty — things that are poems of Nature. But I do not think that he had the instinct which keeps the born countryman uneasy till he can attach himself in permanence to some particular corner of land. His relation to nature was the same in one place as another....'[3]

We get some idea of Osborne's method of work from the letters he wrote home in 1884-5. He would settle in some small town or village where cheap lodgings were to be had, and which offered suitable motifs:

> 'I have an eye on one or two splendid subjects here for pictures and will return, I think.'[4]

He generally worked with another painter or group of painters. No doubt these shifting communities were a factor in the spread of influences, though these are difficult to pin down. It is impossible to tell, for example, to what extent Edward Stott influenced Osborne or vice-versa when they worked together in 1884-1885.

The influence of Bastien-Lepage is apparent, though Osborne did not take wholeheartedly to his rather flashy technique. Bastien worked out of doors:

> 'everything being painted on the spot in a grey light, in order that there might be as little change in the effect as possible while the artist was at work.'[5]

This evenness of lighting is apparent in many of Osborne's early works — see, for example, *The Poachers* (Cat. No. 21), but he was not consistent about it, and he later abandoned it altogether. Paintings like *Loiterers* (Cat. No. 27) or *Punch and Judy on the Sands, Hastings* (Cat. No. 40) gain a great deal of their effect from the dramatic fall of sunlight on a particular part of the picture.

André Theuriet has described Bastien in 1883:

> Muffled in a warm jacket and a travelling cloak that covered him down to the feet, he made his models pose for him in the piercing days of February.[6]

This seems very close to Osborne at North Littleton in 1884:

> The weather I am sorry to say has been bitterly cold the last week, so much so that my model nearly fainted and I had to send her home. I don't mind it a bit myself now I have got on those substantial and very roomy boots.[7]

Osborne also adopted, on occasion, the 'square brush' technique of Bastien Lepage and his followers, see, for example his *Boy under Trees* (Cat. No. 30). He was, however, too much of a draughtsman to allow the paint to take over to the extent that Bastien did. His technique generally comes closer to the Hague School, where brushstrokes are used rather to model the form than run counter to it.

One of the outstanding features of Osborne's work is his technical mastery — he worked confidently and competently in oil, water colour, pastel and pencil. In his oils alone he had a remarkable range — as can be seen even within the fairly limited variety of subject matter of his English *plein air* period.

16 A Vegetable Garden c.1882-4

Oil on board, 20.3 x 25.4 cm. (8 x 10 ins.)

Signed, bottom left: **F. W. Osborne**

PROVENANCE: Mrs. Ruth Jameson Bequest 1979. N.G.I. Cat. No. 4332.

LITERATURE: Sheehy, (1974), no. 28.

This picture is difficult to date — the child's bonnet suggests England, yet the signature is one Osborne used very early in his Antwerp days. There is a touch of the naturalist 'square brush' in the treatment of the cabbages, which are, in themselves an emblem of *plein air* painting, their distinctive blue green is to be seen in many paintings of the naturalist school.

Lent by the National Gallery of Ireland

17   An Artist Sketching
c.1884-5

Oil on board, 22.9 x 12.7 cm. (9 x 5 ins.)

Inscribed, verso: *At Walberswick, an artist sketching. This is a sketch of Nathaniel Hill RHA by his friend Walter Osborne given by the latter to J.B.S. McIlwaine RHA*

PROVENANCE: Presented by the artist to J.B.S. McIlwaine.

EXHIBITED: *Irish Art in the 19th century,* Crawford Art Gallery, Cork, 1971, (112).

LITERATURE: Sheehy, (1974), no. 86.

Hill was a fellow pupil of Osborne's at the schools of the R.H.A. He studied with him at Antwerp, and the two also worked together in Brittany. They were together again at North Littleton in 1884, with Edward Stott. It is possible that the two young painters were at Walberswick because their teacher from the Royal Hibernian Academy Schools, Augustus Burke, was working there at the same period.[8] Wilson Steer later remembered meeting Hill and Osborne there in the eighties.

The 'square brush' of the *plein air* painters is in evidence here, with its interlocking blocks of colour.

Lent by Lord Killanin

18 An October Morning *1885*

Oil, 71.1 x 91.4 cm. (28 x 36 ins.)

Signed and dated, bottom right: **Walter Osborne 1885**

PROVENANCE: Presented to the Corporation of London Art Gallery, the Guildhall, by a group of artists 'as a memorial of the esteem and regard in which the late Walter Osborne was held by them' (see page 10).

EXHIBITED: probably *October by the Sea* exhibited N.E.A.C., 1887, (79); R.H.A., 1888, (49), £50; *Autumn Exhibition,* Walker Art Gallery, Liverpool, 1888, (986), £40; *Works of Irish Painters,* Guildhall, London, 1904, (161); *Post-Impressionism,* R.A., 1979-80, (327).

LITERATURE: Sheehy, (1974), no. 105; Exhibition catalogue (see above), *Post-Impressionism,* p. 204, (327).

Painted at Walberswick, where Osborne was working with Hill, and where he first met Wilson Steer who also used the pier as a motif. This is one of the rare paintings where Osborne adopts an impressionist, indeed almost a divisionist technique. The pebbles are rendered as bright dots of pure colour, though in combination with Osborne's more usual palette of greys and beiges. This was a technique used more often by Stott.[9] To judge by the places at which he exhibited this picture, Osborne considered it important. It has many of the characteristics of his more finished works — a carefully worked out composition, the figures solidly drawn, obviously from preparatory sketches, and set in a framework of still-life detail such as the fish and creels in the foreground.

Lent by The Guildhall Art Gallery, Corporation of London.

Cat. No. 19 — *Feeding Chickens*

19 Feeding Chickens *
1884-5

Oil on canvas, 89.2 x 69 cm. (35½ x 27½ ins.)

Signed and dated, bottom left: **Walter Osborne -85**

PROVENANCE: McCulloch Collection, sold London 1911 for 56 gns; formerly Mr. Shaw, Rathgar.

EXHIBITED: *Winter Exhibition,* Royal Academy, London, 1909, as part of the McCulloch collection of Modern Art; *Works of Irish Painters,* Guildhall, London, 1904, (39).

LITERATURE: Sheehy, (1974), no. 83.

Walter Osborne wrote home to his father from North Littleton, near Evesham, where he was working with Hill and Stott, describing this picture. The letter is dated Sunday Oct. 12th - 84.

> 'Now I am pretty far advanced on a kit-cat of a girl in a sort of farmyard, a rough sketch on the opposite page will indicate the composition. The figure of the girl which is a little over two feet high is coming towards finish, but the immediate foreground with poultry is merely sketched in as yet. The fowl are very troublesome, and I have made some sketches but will have to do a lot more as they form rather an important part of the composition'[10]. (fig. 7)

Fig. 7

The girl's name was Bessie Osborne (apparently quite a common name in those parts, and no relation), and she was painted in the open in weather so cold that she nearly fainted and had to be sent home. The picture is remarkably similar in theme and composition to work of the same period by Stott and Clausen, or by Blandford Fletcher, another of Osborne's painting companions of the period.

The painting seems to have gone straight into the McCulloch Collection, since there is no sign of its being publicly exhibited before 1909. The collection was the one for which George McCulloch built a mansion at 184 Queen's Gate, London, in 1895. It illustrated 'the best phases of British art in the latter half of the nineteenth century', though he also bought works by continental artists. The collection included work by Bastien-Lepage, Dagnan Bouveret, and the Hague School painter Mathew Maris, as well as many British *plein air* painters like Stott, Clausen, La Thangue, Forbes, Garstin and Bramley.[11]

*Not exhibited in the Ulster Museum.

Private Collection

20 Edward Stott
(1855-1918)

Feeding the Ducks *1885*

Oil on canvas, 48 x 39.4 cm. (18⅞ x 15½ ins.)

Signed and dated, bottom right: **Edward Stott 85.**

This was probably painted at the same time as *Feeding Chickens* (Cat. No. 19), when Osborne and Stott were working together.

Lent by City of Manchester Art Galleries

21   The Poachers *1884-5*

Oil on canvas, 49.5 x 68.5 cm. (19½ x 27 ins.)

Signed, bottom left: **Walter Osborne**

PROVENANCE: Miss Violet Stockley, to the present owner by descent.

EXHIBITED: R.H.A., 1885, (58), 40 gns; *Autumn Exhibition*, Walker Art Gallery, Liverpool, 1885, (1003), £30. There is a label on the back saying 'Wherwell, nr. Andover, Hants, £30' — though it is not clear whether the painting was executed there, or merely sent back there from Liverpool. The £30 would suggest the latter. Stott was also working at Wherwell in 1885.[12]

LITERATURE: *Dublin University Review, Illustrated Art Supplement,* (1885); Sheehy, (1974), no. 85.

Like October Morning (Cat. No. 18) this painting shows signs of having been executed from careful pencil studies. The rural subject matter, and the subdued greens of the palette are characteristic of much *plein air* painting of the period. Children and animals were among Osborne's favourite *motifs*.

Lent by Mrs Sophia Mallin

22 The Sheepfold *c.1885*

Oil on board, 33 x 40.6 cm. (13 x 16 ins.)

Signed, bottom left: **Walter Osborne**

PROVENANCE: Formerly collection of John A. Costello

LITERATURE: Sheehy, (1974), no. 107.

Osborne did a series of paintings on this theme — one of them is dated 21/4/85. They are small studies, and are painted with a vividness and clarity that is sometimes missing from the more finished pictures destined for the major exhibitions.

Private Collection

23 Down an Old Court, Newbury *1887*

Oil on board, 23.5 x 15.2 cm. (9½ x 6 ins.)

Signed and dated, bottom left: **Walter Osborne -87.**

PROVENANCE: Formerly collection of Dr. Karl Mullen.

EXHIBITED: Dublin Arts Club, 1887, (161), 7 gns; Irish Painting in the 19th Century, Crawford Art Gallery, Cork, 1971, (113).

LITERATURE: Sheehy, (1974), no. 157.

Osborne was working at this period in small villages in Oxfordshire, Berkshire and Hampshire. At Newbury one of his companions was Blandford Fletcher, a fellow pupil from Antwerp. The painting uses the warm reds to which he was very much attached at this period.

Lent by Mr & Mrs Mervyn Solomon

75

24 A Cottage Garden
1888

Oil on canvas, 67 x 49 cm. (27 x 20 ins.)

Signed, bottom right: **Walter Osborne**

PROVENANCE: Mrs. Catterson Smith, from whom purchased 1912. N.G.I. Cat. No. 635.

EXHIBITED: Possibly *A Bachelor's Garden* exhibited R.H.A., 1889, (46), 35 gns; *Autumn Exhibition,* Royal Birmingham Society, 1889, (221), 25 gns; *Memorial Exhibition,* R.H.A., 1903-04, (125), entitled *An English Garden,* lent by Mrs Catterson Smith.

LITERATURE: Strickland (1913), p. 207, 'painted at Uffington in 1888'; Sheehy, (1974), no. 186.

Osborne seems to have been at Uffington from the summer of 1888. Blandford Fletcher joined him there in the autumn — he did a drawing of Fletcher, in a characteristic pipe-smoking pose, dated 23/11/88.[13] It is an unusual subject for Osborne — he was more a landscape than a flower man — it comes closer to Fletcher's work, and to the English watercolour tradition that we associate with Myles Birket Foster or Helen Allingham.

The bearded figure is thought not to be Camille Pissarro.

Lent by the National Gallery of Ireland

76

25   Near Didcot
c.1886-87

Oil on panel, 23 x 12.7 cm. (9 x 5 ins.)

PROVENANCE: Miss Violet Stockley, to the present owner by descent.

LITERATURE: Stephen Gwynn, *Garden Wisdom*, (1921), p. 35; Sheehy, (1974), no. 183.

Gwynn, who was at Brasenose College, Oxford 1882-1886, wrote 'Another year he was at Byberry, under the clumps which one knows on the skyline from Oxford'.

Lent by Mrs Sophia Mallin

26 A Shepherd and his Flock *1887*

Oil on board, 39.4 x 21.8 cm. (15½ x 12½ ins.)

Signed and dated, bottom left: **Walter Osborne -87.**

PROVENANCE: Formerly collection of Mrs Parker.

LITERATURE: Sheehy, (1974), no. 152.

Many of the paintings of this period are of agricultural pursuits — once again very like Stott, Clausen and La Thangue.

Private Collection

27   Loiterers *1888*

Oil on panel, 35.5 x 25.4 cm. (14 x 10 ins.)

Signed and dated, bottom right: **Walter Osborne -88.**

EXHIBITED: R.H.A., 1889, (220), 15 gns; I.P.O.C., (14); *The Irish Revival,* Pyms Gallery, London, 1982, (2).

LITERATURE: Sheehy, (1974), no. 220.

Another characteristic rural subject, probably, given the date, painted at Uffington. Characteristic of Osborne, too, is the way in which he has articulated the composition with the ray of sunlight that falls across the road, and the sun that still touches the cottage roofs and distant downs.

Lent by Pyms Gallery, London

28   The Lock Gates
c.1888

Oil on canvas, 48.2 x 66 cm. (19½ x 26½ ins.)

EXHIBITED: R.H.A., 1888, (93), 30 gns;
Autumn Exhibition, Walker Art Gallery,
Liverpool, 1888, (186), 30 gns.

LITERATURE: Sheehy, (1974), no. 187.

This painting is in many ways a
compendium of the characteristics of
the English paintings of the late
eighties — the rural genre subject, the
boy and the horse, and the reddish
palette.

Private Collection

29 Fast Falls the Eventide *1888*

Pen and ink, 33.7 x 24.2 cm. (13¾ x 9½ ins.)

Signed, bottom left: **Walter Osborne.**

PROVENANCE: Cynthia O'Connor Gallery, 1981. The painting (untraced) was exhibited at the N.E.A.C., 1888, (7); R.H.A., 1889, (11), 25 gns.

LITERATURE: Henry Blackburn, *Academy Sketches,* (1888), p. 199; Sheehy, (1974), no. 202.

This is typical of the drawings made by painters after their own works especially for inclusion in such publications as Blackburn's *Academy Sketches.* Note the square signature affected by many of the British naturalists in imitation of Bastien-Lepage. The draughtsmanship, too, is similar to that of Stott or Clausen in drawings made for the same purpose.

Lent by Mr W. M. Roth

81

30 Boy under Trees
1887

Oil on panel, 28 x 17.8 cm. (11 x 17 ins.)

Signed and dated, bottom left: **Walter Osborne -87.**

PROVENANCE: Formerly collection of Violet Stockley.

LITERATURE: Sheehy, (1974), no. 158.

Another small, rural picture, very conscious of its handling. Here Osborne is using more systematically than usual the 'square brush' technique associated with Bastien-Lepage and his imitators among the English naturalists.

Private Collection

31   A Boy in a Turnip Field *1888*

Oil on board, 14 x 22.9 cm. (5½ x 9 ins.)

Signed and dated, bottom left: **Walter Osborne -88.**

PROVENANCE: Stephen Gwynn to the present owner by descent.

LITERATURE: Stephen Gwynn *Garden Wisdom,* (1921), p. 41; Sheehy, (1974), no. 178.

Gwynn wrote
'But in the little green picture on the right, the stillness is of midsummer; a line of Berkshire Downs rises beyond a turnip field which a boy is thinning, and beyond are little vaporous balls of cloud, white edged, that float without apparent motion:

If the painting was done in the summer of 1888, then presumably it is one of the Uffington pictures.

Lent by Mrs Alice Gwynn

32   Ploughing *1887-88?*

Oil on board, 30.5 x 38.1 cm. (12 x 15 ins.)

Signed, bottom left: **Walter Osborne.**

LITERATURE: Sheehy, (1974), no. 154.

This is a theme which Osborne treated several times in his English period. It is interesting to compare it to Clausen's famous *Ploughing* (Fig. No. 6), exhibited at the *Grosvenor Gallery* in 1889, and at the winter exhibition of the *Dublin Arts Club* in 1890.[15] Though the basic ingredients of the two paintings are much the same, Clausen treats his landscape as a background to his animals and people, and the boy, in particular, is treated as a personality. With Osborne the animals and men are elements in the landscape.

Private Collection

33 Potato Gathering
1888

Oil on board, 31.8 x 38.1 cm. (12½ x 15 ins.)

Signed, bottom left: **Walter Osborne**

PROVENANCE: By descent.

EXHIBITED: Dublin Art Club, 1889, (30), 30 gns.

LITERATURE: Sheehy, (1974), no. 180.

The theme is reminiscent of Bastien-Lepage's *Saison d'Octobre*,[16] though the comparison once again underlines the difference between Osborne and the French naturalist tradition. Bastien is concerned, in a way that recalls Millet, with the condition of the labourer, whereas Osborne is more interested in the rural activity as part of the landscape.

Private Collection

34 Landscape with Crows *c.1888-90*

Oil on board, 41.9 x 26.7 cm. (16½ x 10½ ins.)

PROVENANCE: Canon C. E. Osborne Bequest, 1971.

LITERATURE: Sheehy, (1974), no. 253.

This is an excellent example of Osborne's skill with tone and colour in the handling of space. The picture has such simple elements, and yet the articulation of the landscape is confident and precise, and the colour subtle.

Lent by The Hugh Lane Municipal Gallery of Modern Art, Dublin

35 Harvest Time
c.1890

Oil on canvas, 38.1 x 30.5 cm. (15 x 12 ins.)

Signed, bottom left: **Walter Osborne.**

PROVENANCE: W. E. Purser (who probably bought it from the painter) to the present owner by descent.

EXHIBITED: *Autumn Exhibition,* Royal Birmingham Society, 1891, (537), 15 gns; R.H.A., 1892, (261), 15 gns; *Memorial Exhibition,* R.H.A., 1903-04, (10), lent by W. E. Purser Esq.

LITERATURE: Sheehy, (1974), no. 236.

This mellow autumn landscape is an indication of the extent to which Osborne's interests were not social or topographical, but rather in the changing seasons and their impact on agricultural and country life — and more than anything else in the ways in which these things could be rendered in paint on canvas.

Private Collection

36 Joe the Swineherd
1890

Oil on canvas, 50.8 x 68.6 cm. (20 x 27 ins.)

Signed and dated, bottom left: **Walter Osborne -90.**

PROVENANCE: By descent.

EXHIBITED: R.A., 1891, (613); *Autumn Exhibition,* Walker Art Gallery, Liverpool, 1891, (1155), 40 gns; R.H.A., 1892, (87), 30 gns.

LITERATURE: Sheehy, (1974), no. 234.

It is interesting how Osborne's background as an animal painter, derived from the influence of his father and his training under Verlat at Antwerp, persists, so that the paintings of this period are littered with pigs, sheep, horses, cows and dogs. According to Stephen Gwynn 'it was a grievance of his that pictures with sheep for their chief feature were difficult to sell, and pigs commercially quite impossible: I think some black Berkshire yearlings rooting about in a golden stubble, stayed, unsold, with him to the end'.[17]

Private Collection

37   Cherry Ripe *c.1889*

Oil on canvas, 68.5 x 50.5 cm. (27 x 20 ins.)

Signed, bottom right: **Walter Osborne**

PROVENANCE: Beaux Arts Gallery, London, from whom purchased, 1951.

EXHIBITED: I.P.O.C., 1889-90, (300), £50.

LITERATURE: *Boy's Own Paper,* June (1895); *Magazine of Art,* (1890), p. 114; Sheehy, (1974), no. 210.

The painting is now exhibited as *Street Scene at Sunset.* Perhaps the sentimentality of the original title is out of keeping with modern taste, though it is not out of keeping with the character of Osborne's work, when one considers his fondness for children and animals. There is also a degree to which Osborne's titles are more sentimental than the pictures themselves, which are sharply observed and rendered with the 'truth' so much valued by the naturalist painters. This painting is an instance of the care which Osborne put into the composition of a picture — there exist a pencil sketch of the street, and a fully finished watercolour of the same place. Another painting, showing the man with the donkey, was exhibited in 1891. The evidence indicates that his paintings were completed in the studio from studies made in front of the motif.

Lent by the Ulster Museum, Belfast

38   Boat Builders *1889*

Oil on canvas, 34.3 x 44.5 cm. (13½ x 17½ ins.)

Signed and dated, bottom left: **Walter Osborne -89.**

PROVENANCE: Formerly collection of Augustine Orr.

EXHIBITED: I.P.O.C., 1889-90, (243), £25; R.H.A., 1890, (199), £25; *Memorial Exhibition,* R.H.A., 1903-04, (112), lent by Augustine Orr, Esq.

LITERATURE: Sheehy, (1974), no. 205.

In the period of his early maturity Osborne worked not only in rural areas, but also by the sea. As we have seen he worked at Walberswick around 1884-5. In the later eighties and early nineties he worked on the south coast, at Rye and Hastings. This may have been because his brother Charles was assistant curate to Father Dolling at Landport, Portsmouth, 1886-93.

Here we have the seaside equivalent of the rural pictures, including, as usual, children.

Private Collection

39　The Ferry, *Sketch*
1889-90.

Oil on panel, 32 x 30 cm. (13 x 12 ins.)

PROVENANCE: Herbert Hone (purchased from the Trustees of Osborne's estate by Nathaniel Hone), to the present owner by descent.

EXHIBITED: *Memorial Exhibition,* R.H.A., 1903-04, (189), lent by the Trustees of Osborne's estate.

LITERATURE: Sheehy, (1974), no. 207.

This is related to *The Ferry* (present whereabouts unknown), a picture well known and much reproduced in Osborne's own time, which won him a bronze medal at the Worlds Columbian Exhibition, Chicago, 1893. The study of boats also suggests a relationship to *Boat Builders* (Cat. No. 38), another one of the group of seaside pictures of the late eighties.

Lent by Mr David Hone

40   Punch and Judy on the Sands, Hastings *1891-2*

Oil on canvas, 33 x 40.5 cm. (12½ x 15½ ins.)

Signed, bottom left: **Walter Osborne.**

PROVENANCE: Collection of Rt. Hon. Lord
Justice O'Connor; E. V. Huxtable by whom
presented, 1924. N.G.I. Cat. No. 858.

EXHIBITED: R.H.A., 1892, (280), 20 gns;
Ierse Schilders der 19ᵉ en 20ᵉ eeuw, Stedlijk
Museum, Amsterdam, 1951, (29); *Lane
Bequest Exhibition*, Ulster Museum, Belfast,
1970-71; *The Architecture of Ireland in
Drawings and Paintings*, N.G.I., 1975, (70).

LITERATURE: Sheehy, (1974), no. 273.

This painting is called *A View of
Hastings* at the National Gallery. The
original title is an indication of the way
in which Osborne's titles can be
misleading, and suggest an anecdotal
emphasis missing from the paintings
themselves. The main interest in this
picture is not what is going on on the
beach, but rather the light falling on
the distant houses. This is emphasised
by the notes on the pencil sketch
related to this work (see next entry).

Lent by the National Gallery of Ireland

92

41   Hastings *1891*

Pencil on white paper, 25.6 x 17.8 cm. (10 x 7 ins.)

Inscribed, bottom right: **Hastings 2/11/91.**

PROVENANCE: Purchased from the artist's executors. N.G.I. Cat. No. 2538.

LITERATURE: Sheehy, (1974), no. 274.

A pencil study related to the previous entry. The notes on it are an interesting indication of Osborne's method of work: 'clouds working up. Sky green through warm clouds, cold at base. Glow on houses'.

Lent by the National Gallery of Ireland

42 A Seaside Promenade *c.1891*

Oil on board, 12.7 x 16.5 cm. (5 x 6½ ins.)

PROVENANCE: Purchased from Osborne's estate, formerly collection of E. A. McGuire.

LITERATURE: Sheehy, (1974), no. 275.

There is a Whistlerian spareness about this picture which links it to his later work. The suggestion is of bright summer sunshine, as opposed to the wintry light of *Punch and Judy* (Cat. No. 40).

Ireland: Landscape and Genre

Ireland: Landscape and Genre

Osborne's painting underwent a number of changes in the 1890s, after he ceased to work in England. There are various reasons for this. The major one is that he was no longer primarily a landscape and genre painter, but was turning increasingly to portraiture. This aspect of his career will be discussed in the next section. Inevitably the changes in his environment began to affect his pictures — he was painting in different places and he was mixing with different people. These changes did not happen suddenly. There is considerable overlap between the kind of picture he was painting in England in the eighties, and his Irish work of the nineties. Some of the later work — *The Thornbush* of 1893-4 (Cat. No. 46) for example, can be related in both subject matter and treatment to the *plein air* pictures he did in England in the company of men like Edward Stott. The Dublin market pictures of the nineties, though they belong to the same tradition, are different. They show a greater interest in people, more involvement in their lives, than most of Osborne's early work. Many Realist and Naturalist painters tried to come to terms, in their painting, with the people of their own native place, for example Courbet with Ornans, and Bastien-Lepage with Damvillers, and it is as if the Dublin streets fulfilled this function for Osborne.[1] It is largely a matter of subject matter — his method of work did not change in the early to mid nineties. He still made dozens of pencil sketches, studies of individual figures or of genre detail, and some oil sketches, and then worked the whole lot up in the studio to achieve the finished composition. See, for example, the pencil study for *Life in the Streets, Musicians* (Cat. No. 50) or *In a Dublin Park, Light and Shade,* and the various studies related to it (Cat. Nos. 52-55).

But his manner of painting also began to change. In his later work his palette is more adventurous, his brushwork looser, and his approach more painterly. One no longer has the feeling that the figures have been worked out separately in careful preparatory drawings, they are much more integrated into the painting. Compare, for example, *The Lustre Jug* (Cat. No. 74) or *The Housebuilders* (Cat. No. 75) with *Near St Patrick's Close* (Cat. No. 44) of 1887. It was once fashionable to attribute all such changes to the influence of French Impressionism, just as it is now fashionable to deplore the ascendancy attributed to the Parisian avant-garde. Osborne was not an Impressionist — his way of making a picture and his attitude to his subject matter are different from theirs, but he must certainly have been influenced by them. There can be no other way of accounting for the luminous colour to be found in the late interiors such as *The Lustre Jug* (Cat. No. 74) or the vivid boldness of *Galway Fair* (Cat. No. 61) or *On the Beach* (Cat. No. 77). The influence of Impressionism may have come directly from Monet and Degas, both of whom exhibited at the New English Art Club. Osborne made a small sketch and colour notes of a design for a fan Degas exhibited there in 1893 (Cat. No. 101). There is a draughtsmanlike precision about Osborne's work that has more in common with Degas than with Monet. French Impressionist influence will also have come through the English Impressionists of the New English — Steer and Brown and Sickert. Osborne knew, Steer, whom he had met at Walberswick in the early eighties,[2] and he owned a painting by Brown.[3] One should also remember that *plein air* painters like Clausen and Stott also came under Impressionist influence in their later work.

Various other influences also contributed to Osborne's growing painterliness, his tendency to treat forms as related areas of paint rather than emphasising the underlying drawing. He admired Manet, one of the few modern French painters he was prepared to praise when he visited the Luxembourg in 1895.[4] Whistler, too, had long been a favourite of his — he made a sketch after a Whistler portrait as early as 1884 (Cat. No. 99) and he did a charming drawing after *Miss Cicely Alexander* (Cat. No. 106) at the Dublin Art Loan Exhibition of 1899. An increasing economy of detail and daring in composition, such as in *Galway Fair* (Cat. No. 61) probably owe a good deal to Whistler's influence. His friendship with Armstrong also introduced him to Spanish painting, and he conceived a great enthusiasm for Velázquez and for Goya, both painterly painters with a powerful command of subtle harmonies.

Walter Osborne's subjects did not change completely during the latter part of his career. We still find rustic genre scenes with animals — for example the sketch for *Milking Time in St Marnock's Byre* (Cat. No. 68), views of village streets, and straight landscapes. In appearance, however, they are different from the early work of the same kind — more broadly and boldly handled, more adventurous in colour. As paintings they are direct and personal, less dependent on other painters as models. This is a painter in full control of his medium and his expression. He might, in his portraits, have become 'the kind of Salon virtuoso into which Sargent too often degenerated',[5] but in his other work he had clearly just embarked on a new and fruitful phase of his artistic career.

43 In St. Patrick's Cathedral *1887*

Oil on canvas, 27.3 x 29 cm. (10¾ x 15½ ins.)

Signed and dated, bottom left: **Walter Osborne -87.**

EXHIBITED: Possibly *St Patrick's Cathedral, Memorial Exhibition,* R.H.A., 1903-04, lent by G. Dixon; or *Captain Boyd's Monument, St Patrick's* in the same exhibition, lent by W. Booth Pearsall, H.R.H.A.

This painting shows that Osborne was already becoming interested in the life of the Dublin streets when he was still spending much of his time painting in England. The monument, by Thomas Farrell, is to Captain John McNeil Boyd, who lost his life in a rescue attempt off Dun Laoghaire.[6] The church interior recalls those of the Hague School painter Bosboom, though the scale is more intimate and the genre element stronger than is usually to be found in the church interiors of the Dutch School.

Private Collection

44 Near St. Patrick's Close, an Old Dublin Street *1887*

Oil on canvas 69 x 51 cm. (27 x 20 ins.)

Signed and dated, bottom left: **Walter Osborne 1887**

PROVENANCE: Mrs. E. Fitzgerald, from whom purchased, 1921. N.G.I. Cat. No. 836.

EXHIBITED: R.A., 1887, (387), £50; *Autumn Exhibition,* Walker Art Gallery, Liverpool, 1887, (298), £50; R.H.A., 1888, (95), 40 gns; *Ierse Schilders der 19e en 20e eeuw,* Stedelijk Museum, Amsterdam, 1951, (28); *Painting in England and Ireland, 1700-1900,* Marist Hall, Dundalk, 1970, (22); *Aspects of Irish Art,* Columbus Gallery of Fine Arts, Toledo Museum of Arts, St. Louis Art Museum, 1974, (61); *The Architecture of Ireland in Drawings and Paintings,* N.G.I., 1975, (69).

LITERATURE: *Academy Sketches,* (1887), p. 66; T. McGreevy, *National Gallery Illustrated Catalogue,* (1945), p. 46; *Phaidon Companion to Art and Artists in the British Isles,* (1980), p. IR 18; Sheehy, (1974), no. 151; *National Gallery of Ireland, 50 Pictures,* (1982).

The title of this picture is somewhat misleading, since the view is along Patrick Street with the vista closed by the tower which stands at the north side of the west front of St Patrick's Cathedral. It is the earliest of a series of pictures of the market area of Dublin which Osborne continued to paint in the nineties. The evocation of the smoke laden atmosphere of the wintry street is more successful than the piping boy in the foreground.

Lent by the National Gallery of Ireland

45 Patrick Street, Dublin *c.1892*

Pencil on white paper, 25 x 17.5 cm. (10 x 7 ins.)

PROVENANCE: Purchased from the artist's executors, 1903. N.G.I. Cat. No. 2539.

LITERATURE: Sheehy, (1974), no. 332.

This view looks back up Patrick Street towards Christ Church Cathedral. The drawing is related to Osborne's pastel *Life in the Streets, Hard Times* which was exhibited at the Royal Academy in 1892 and bought under the terms of the Chantrey Bequest. It is now in the Tate Gallery, London.

Lent by the National Gallery of Ireland

46 The Thornbush *1893-4*

Oil on canvas, 71.1 x 91.4 cm. (28 x 36 ins.)

Signed and dated, bottom left: **Walter Osborne -94.**

PROVENANCE: Collection of Barrington Jellett; sold at the auction of paintings belonging to Canon Harris 3rd April 1914; Dr. Cremin, to the present owner by descent.

EXHIBITED: R.A., 1894, (43); R.H.A., 1895, (47), 50 gns; *Exposition d'Art Irlandais,* Brussels, 1930, (20), lent by Dr. Cremin; *Irish International Exhibition,* Dublin, 1907, (73).

LITERATURE: Strickland, (1913), p. 206, 'Painted at Foxrock in 1893'; *Academy Notes;* (1894); Sheehy, (1974), no. 359.

When Osborne ceased working in England he turned for landscape motifs to Co. Dublin, generally places like Portmarnock and Malahide, to the north of the city. Sometimes he visited his friend J. B. S. MacIlwaine, who had a house at Foxrock. Beatrice Elvery remembered seeing him at work near the quarry holes at Foxrock, painting animals and the children from the cottages. There is a study of goats in the Hugh Lane Municipal Gallery of Modern Art inscribed 'Foxrock 10/9/92'. This picture is not at all unlike his *plein air* paintings of the

previous decade, with its sober palette and careful composition, and uneventful scenery peopled by children and animals.

Lent by Mrs C. M. Cremin

47   Cows in a Field
1892

Oil on canvas, 36 x 51 cm. (13½ x 19 ins.)

Signed and dated, bottom left: **Walter Osborne -92.**

PROVENANCE: Stephen Gwynn; Mrs T. Moorehead, by whom presented, 1978. N.G.I. Cat. No. 4314.

LITERATURE: Sheehy, (1974), no. 318.

It is curious that, though Osborne painted sheep and pigs, horses and dogs while he was in England, he hardly ever painted cows, whereas he painted cattle a great deal in the Irish phase of his career. This may have been due to the influence of Nathaniel Hone, with whom he became friendly. Hone produced a large number of landscapes with cattle not at all unlike this one, though perhaps more vigorous in handling.

Lent by the National Gallery of Ireland

48   Study of Cattle
c.1892

Pencil on white paper, 17.8 x 25 cm. (7 x 10 ins.)

PROVENANCE: Purchased from the artist's executors, 1903. N.G.I. Cat. No. 2547.

EXHIBITED: Wexford Festival, 1970.

LITERATURE: Sheehy, (1974), no. 319.

The drawing has notes about the treatment of colour and light: 'Face lower in tone than light over ear x dewlap greeny yellow Jaw dark against grass, greeny white', demonstrating how he used pencil sketches with notes, taken on the spot, to refresh his memory when completing a painting in the studio. He also generally made oil sketches on the spot.

Lent by the National Gallery of Ireland

49   Life in the Streets, Musicians *1893*

Oil on canvas, 59.7 x 80 cm. (23½ x 31½ ins.)

Signed and dated, bottom left: **Walter Osborne -93.**

PROVENANCE: Lane Gift, 1912.

EXHIBITED: R.A., 1894, (823); *Autumn Exhibition,* Walker Art Gallery, Liverpool, 1894, (98), 70 gns; *Memorial Exhibition,* R.H.A., 1903-04, (26), lent by the Trustees of Osborne's estate; *Works of Irish Painters,* Guildhall, London, 1904, (185); *Franco-British Exhibition,* London, 1908, (58).

LITERATURE: *Academy Notes,* (1894); Sheehy, (1974), no. 360.

This painting was bought by Lane after Osborne's death, and presented to the Gallery. When Osborne died Lane wrote to Sarah Purser saying that something should be done to secure some of his works for the nation, and lamenting his loss 'It has been a great shock to me as he was one of our few geniuses, and I hoped for still greater things from his brush'.7 It is note-worthy that Osborne's market pictures show more interest in people as individuals, as characters, than his English rural paintings had done. Perhaps, in the Dublin market people

he had found his own equivalent of Bastien's Damvillers peasants or Stanhope Forbes' Cornish fisher folk. There is an interesting combination of techniques in this painting, with its free handling and subtle build up of tones and hues in the background, and the extraordinary nacreous encrusta-tion of colour in the fish-stall. The picture has been titled *The Fishmarket* since it entered the Municipal Gallery.

Lent by the Hugh Lane Municipal Gallery of Modern Art, Dublin

50 Sketch of a Dublin Fishwife *1892-3*

Pencil on white paper, 17.7 x 25.1 cm. (7 x 10 ins.)

PROVENANCE: Purchased from the artist's executors, 1903. N.G.I. Cat. No. 2543.

LITERATURE: Sheehy, (1974), no. 361.

Pencil sketch for the woman in the left foreground of Cat. No. 49. There is a note 'Sketch for street scene Dublin. Fisherwoman in foreground'. Once again we can see the care, and comparative lack of spontaneity with which Osborne built up his pictures, however direct they may sometimes seem.

Lent by the National Gallery of Ireland

51 The Market, Patrick Street *c.1893-5*

Watercolour on white paper, 17.8 x 25.4 cm. (7 x 10 ins.)

Signed, bottom left: **Walter Osborne.**

PROVENANCE: By descent.

EXHIBITED: *Irish Art in the 19th Century,* Crawford Art Gallery, Cork, 1971, (115).

LITERATURE: Sheehy, (1974), no. 428.

Another variant on the market theme. It is clear that Osborne haunted the Patrick Street area during the nineties, and worked in all the media at his disposal — watercolour, oil, pastel and pencil. Apart from the finished compositions there exist a large number of pencil studies for these works — figures singly or in groups, and studies for stalls piled with hats or crockery.

Private Collection

52 In a Dublin Park, Light and Shade *c.1895*

Oil on canvas, 71 x 91 cm. (28½ x 35¾ ins.)

Signed, bottom right: **Walter Osborne.**

PROVENANCE: W.J. McCoughey J.P. Belfast; J. K. Bell, from whom purchased 1944. N.G.I. Cat. No. 1121.

EXHIBITED: R.A., 1895, (782); R.A., 1895, (782); *Aspects of Irish Art,* Colombus Gallery of Fine Arts, Toledo Museum of Arts and St Louis Art Museum, 1974, (62).

LITERATURE: *Royal Academy Pictures;* (1895); *Black and White,* (1895); Sheehy, (1974), no. 419.

One of the rare pictures which Osborne sold when it was first exhibited, since he only seems to have shown it at the Royal Academy. Its popularity is also indicated by the fact that it was illustrated in two of the guides to that year's exhibition.

Of all of his paintings, even his Dublin ones, this is the one in which Osborne shows most involvement in the lives of his sitters, and more interest than usual in matters other than the purely visual — this reads rather like an allegory of life, from babyhood to old age. It is broadly and confidently handled, however, with Osborne's usual sharpness of vision.

Lent by the National Gallery of Ireland

53 Mother and Child
c.1895

Oil on canvas, 44.5 x 34.3 cm. (17¼ x 13¼ ins.)

PROVENANCE: Lane Gift, 1912.

EXHIBITED: *Memorial Exhibition*, R.H.A., 1903-04, (115), lent by the Trustees of Osborne's estate.

LITERATURE: Sheehy, (1974), no. 420.

This is another of the paintings bought by Lane after Osborne's death. It is related to *In a Dublin Park* (Cat. No. 52) using the same tired mother with a baby that we see in that picture, but painted in an interior. Osborne often re-used motifs in this way.

Lent by the Hugh Lane Municipal
Gallery of Modern Art, Dublin

54 Mother and Child
c.1895

Pencil on white paper, 18 x 11.3 cm. (7 x 4½ ins.)

PROVENANCE: Purchased from the artist's executors, 1903. N.G.I. Cat. No. 2544.

EXHIBITED: Wexford Festival, 1970, (41).

LITERATURE: Sheehy, (1974), no. 421.

Study for *In a Dublin Park* (Cat. No. 52).

Lent by the National Gallery of Ireland

55 In St. Stephen's Green

Pencil on white paper, 17.6 x 23.8 cm. (7 x 9½ ins.)

PROVENANCE: Purchased from the artist's executors, 1903. N.G.I. Cat. No. 2549.

EXHIBITED: Wexford Festival, 1970, (41).

LITERATURE: Sheehy, (1974), no. 423.

This is a preliminary study for another of the pictures painted in Dublin parks, and contains the notes about tone and colour familiar from other drawings.

Lent by the National Gallery of Ireland

56   St. Stephen's Green *1895-1900*

Pencil on white paper, 12.7 x 20.3 cm. (5 x 8 ins.)

PROVENANCE: Purchased from the artist's executors, 1903. N.G.I. Cat. No. 2545.

LITERATURE: Sheehy, (1974), no. 424.

The north side of St. Stephen's Green, Dublin, looking towards Merrion Row.

57   St. Stephen's Green *1895-1900*

Pencil on white paper, 12.7 x 20.3 cm. (5 x 8
ins.)

PROVENANCE: Purchased from the artist's
executors, 1903. N.G.I. Cat. No. 2546.

EXHIBITED: Wexford Festival, 1970, (41).

LITERATURE: Sheehy, (1974), no. 425.

To judge from the notations — 'slate',
'red brick, dull' and 'heads near on level
with bottom of distant brick' Osborne
intended to make a painting of this
subject, though it has not come to light.

Lent by the National Gallery of Ireland

58   A Dublin Flower Girl *1895-1900*

Pencil on white paper, 20.3 x 12.8 cm. (8 x 5 ins.)

PROVENANCE: Purchased from the artist's executors, 1903. N.G.I. Cat. No. 2548.

EXHIBITED: Wexford Festival, 1970, (41).

LITERATURE: Sheehy, (1974), no. 427.

It does not seem possible to identify where this was drawn. It is a good example of Osborne's sharpness as a draughtsman — even in this rudimentary drawing the heads of the women are vividly evoked.

Lent by the National Gallery of Ireland

114

59 Marsh's Library, Dublin *1898*

Oil on panel, 38.1 x 30.5 cm. (15 x 12 ins.)

Signed and dated, bottom left: **Walter Osborne -98.**

PROVENANCE: Mrs. J. H. Twigg, (née Alice Hull) Bequest, 1937, through her nephew Surgeon Captain F. J. D. Twigg.

EXHIBITED: As *In a Free Library,* Society of Oil Painters, 1898-9, (176), 45 gns; R.H.A., 1899, (45), £42.

LITERATURE: Sheehy, (1974), no. 485.

One of the two paintings Osborne did inside the library adjoining St. Patrick's Cathedral, founded by Narcissus Marsh at the beginning of the eighteenth century.

Lent by the Hugh Lane Municipal Gallery of Modern Art, Dublin

60   The Four Courts, Dublin *c.1901*

Oil on board, 32.5 x 40.5 cm. (13 x 16 ins.)

Signed, bottom left: **Walter Osborne**

PROVENANCE: Mr A. Thompson, from whom purchased, 1969. N.G.I. Cat. No. 1916.

LITERATURE: Sheehy, (1974), no. 557.

A purely topographical urban view is rare in Osborne's work, though his range of subject widened considerably in the period of just over a decade when he was settled back in Dublin. He gradually abandoned the 'square brush' — this is a late picture in which it is entirely absent — for broader, looser, more varied brushwork, such as we see here. He also abandoned the square signature which was the hallmark of Bastien-Lepage's English followers, and adopted a cursive one based on his own handwriting.

Lent by the National Gallery of Ireland

61 Galway Fair *1893*

Oil on canvas, 17.8 x 27.3 cm. (7 x 10¾ ins.)

Signed and dated, bottom left: **Walter Osborne -93.**

PROVENANCE: Formerly collection of Edmund Lupton.

EXHIBITED: Possibly *The Horse Fair, Galway,* Dublin Arts Club, 1894, (37), 8 gns; *Irish Art in the 19th century,* Crawford Art Gallery, Cork, 1971, (114).

LITERATURE: Sheehy, (1974), no. 362.

As well as painting in Dublin city and county, Osborne also made occasional trips westwards, to Limerick and to Galway where he did a series of market pictures, quite different from the more sober Dublin ones — freely handled and vividly painted. His composition, too, is much less staid, as in this picture with its great blank expanse of foreground and its decorative frieze of figures in the upper part of the picture.

Private Collection

62   A Sketch, Galway *1893*

Pencil on white paper, 17.7 x 25.1 cm. (7 x 10 ins.)

Inscribed: *Galway 2/9/93.*

PROVENANCE: Purchased from the artist's executors, 1903. N.G.I. Cat. No. 2542.

EXHIBITED: Wexford Festival, 1970, (41).

LITERATURE: Sheehy, (1974), no. 366.

A vividly evocative drawing done on the same trip as Cat. No. 61.

Lent by the National Gallery of Ireland

63   Rising Moon, Galway Harbour *c.1893*

Oil on board, 31.7 x 39.4 cm. (12½ x 15½ ins.)

Signed, bottom right: **Walter Osborne**

PROVENANCE: John Jameson; Richard Irvine Best Bequest, through the Friends of the National Collections, 1960.

EXHIBITED: *Memorial Exhibition*, R.H.A., 1903-04, (46), lent by John Jameson.

LITERATURE: Sheehy, (1974), no. 325.

This, once again, is an unusual painting for Osborne. He does not seem to have been attracted by the blue and purple Connemara landscape as so many subsequent Irish painters were. He did, however, make a number of studies of twilight and moonlight, giving him the excuse to deploy rich effects of blue, as here, and in *Starlight* (Cat. No. 71).

Lent by the Hugh Lane Municipal
Gallery of Modern Art, Dublin

119

64 A Galway Cottage *c.1900*

Oil on panel, 30 x 38 cm. (12½ x 15¾ ins.)

signed, top left: **Walter Osborne**

PROVENANCE: Purchased from the artist's
executors, 1903. N.G.I. Cat. No. 554.

EXHIBITED: Probably *In a Connemara
Cottage,* Society of Oil Painters, 1900, (123),
25 gns; R.H.A., 1901, (230), 20 gns; *Ierse
Schilders der 19e en 20e eeuw,* Stedelijk
Museum, Amsterdam, 1951, (26).

LITERATURE: Sheehy, (1974), no. 542.

A return to the rural themes of his
early work, but handled with much
more freedom and richness. The
painting is reminiscent of the Dutch
interiors of Jozef Israëls and other
painters of the Hague School.

Lent by the National Gallery of Ireland

65 The Spanish Trip
1895

A series of drawings mounted together

PROVENANCE: Walter Armstrong; Purchased London, 1966. N.G.I. Cat. No. 3800-3806.

INSCRIBED: *To W. A. from W.O. A souvenir of a little tour in Spain Dec 1895*

LITERATURE: Sheehy, (1974), nos. 453-459.

In 1895 Osborne made a journey through France to Spain with his friend Walter Armstrong, Director of the National Gallery of Ireland 1892-1914. The two stayed in Paris, then went on through Bordeaux to Madrid. In Paris Osborne lamented that he had not got his painting things with him,[8] but he seems to have done a certain amount of sketching on the trip. Several of the drawings, *In the Train, At Brincola* and *Café de Madrid,* show Walter Armstrong.

Algodor, way to Toledo
Pencil, 11 x 17.5 cm. (4¼ x 6⅞ ins.)

Boy in the Café Moka, Madrid
Pencil, 11.8 x 9 cm. (5 x 3¼ ins.)

In the Train
Pencil, 16 x 11 cm. (6¼ x 4¼ ins.)

Lent by the National Gallery of Ireland

At Brincola
Pencil, 12.6 x 7.5 cm. (5 x 3 ins.)

Café de Madrid, Madrid
Pencil, 15 x 10.1 cm. (6 x 4 ins.)

A member of the Orchestra, Palais Royale, Paris
Pencil, 10.6 x 9.57 cm. (4¼ x 3¾ ins.)

Man in a Spanish Hat at the Café Inglese, Madrid
Pencil, 16.1 x 11 cm. (6⅝ x 4¼ ins.)

Lent by the National Gallery of Ireland

66   The Synagogue, Toledo *1895*

Pencil on white paper, 25.5 x 17.6 cm. (10 x 7 ins.)

Inscribed: *The Synagogue. El Transito. 1366. Toledo.*

PROVENANCE: Purchased, London, 1966. N.G.I. Cat. No. 3799.

LITERATURE: Sheehy, (1974), no. 460.

Lent by the National Gallery of Ireland

67   A New Year Greeting *1894*

Pen and ink on writing paper, 16.5 x 10.2 cm. (6½ x 4 ins.)

The paper has the letterhead of 5 Castlewood Avenue, and is inscribed: *With best wishes from Walter Osborne.*

PROVENANCE: Formerly collection of Dr. Karl Mullen

LITERATURE: Sheehy, (1974), no. 400.

This demonstrates two facets of Osborne's character, his love of animals, and his sense of fun, which many people who knew him spoke about.

Lent by Dr. Dermot Walsh

124

68   Milking Time *c.1898*

Oil on canvas, 19 x 28 cm. (7½ x 11 ins.)

PROVENANCE: Formerly collection of John Jameson.

EXHIBITED: *Memorial Exhibition*, R.H.A., 1903-04, (225), lent by John Jameson.

LITERATURE: Sheehy, (1974), no. 488.

During the later part of his life Osborne used to take a cottage in the summer in north Co. Dublin, at Portmarnock or Malahide.[9] He had friends in the area — Nathaniel Hone at Malahide, and the Jamesons at St. Marnock's. He did several cattle paintings for the Jamesons — two finished works *Milking Time in St. Marnock's Byre*, and *Cattle, St. Marnock's*. This is probably a sketch for the former. The existence of such studies is an indication that Osborne still prepared his pictures with great care, but there is much more directness and vigour in his later work. It is not that a move towards a more impressionist handling is necessarily better of itself, but that the later paintings have a directness and confidence that the earlier ones lacked. Osborne was by now a mature painter, sure of his medium, and of his responses.

Lent by Lord Killanin

69 Cattle in the Sea
c.1898

Oil on board, 19 x 25 cm. (7½ x 11 ins.)

PROVENANCE: Formerly collection of Herbert Hone.

EXHIBITED: *Memorial Exhibition*, R.H.A., 1903-04, (251), lent by Nathaniel Hone R.H.A.

LITERATURE: Sheehy, (1974), no. 492.

This shows cattle on the Velvet Strand at St. Marnock's, and may be a sketch for the other Jameson picture (see Cat. No. 68). It is interesting that it should have belonged to Nathaniel Hone, whose own cattle pictures have an attack that may have affected Osborne's work. Hone was trained in Paris under Couture.

Private Collection

70 Sketch at Malahide
c.1898

Oil on canvas, 31 x 38.7 cm. (12¼ x 15¼ ins.)

PROVENANCE: Guinness Collection.

LITERATURE: Sheehy, (1974), no. 495.

One of a pair of very simple paintings of beach and sea, said to have been done by Osborne at the request of Mrs. Noel Guinness, whose portrait he painted (Cat. No. 90).

Lent from the Guinness Collection

71   Starlight *c.1898*

Oil on canvas, 50.8 x 61 cm. (20 x 24 ins.)

Signed, bottom left: **Walter Osborne**

PROVENANCE: Formerly collection of Andrew Jameson.

EXHIBITED: *Memorial Exhibition,* R.H.A., 1903-04, (94), lent by Andrew Jameson; *Irish International Exhibition,* Dublin, 1907, entitled *Moonlight,* lent by Andrew Jameson.

LITERATURE: Sheehy, (1974), no. 500.

A daring experiment, showing the village street at Rush, Co. Dublin, with a starry sky, and light streaming from doors and windows. The predominant blues and browns with which the painter achieves the effect of night are lit up occasionally by vivid flashes of yellow and red, and the luminous glow of the cottage walls is particularly effective. The powdering of small regular brushstrokes is unusual in Osborne's work, and closer to the technique of Edward Stott or Clausen at the end of the century. Osborne has handled a difficult subject with complete success.

Private Collection

72   At A Child's Bedside *1898*

Watercolour, 17.8 x 25.4 cm. (7 x 10 ins.)

Signed, bottom left: **Walter Osborne**

Inscribed, verso: *Painted in September 1898 when Violet was 5 years of age.*

PROVENANCE: Miss Violet Stockley, to the present owner by descent.

EXHIBITED: N.E.A.C., 1899, (30); *Memorial Exhibition,* R.H.A., 1903-04, (72), lent by Mrs Osborne.

LITERATURE: Sheehy, (1974), no. 507.

The child is Violet Stockley, the painter's niece, who figures in a great many of his later paintings. The extent to which he used watercolour increasingly in his later work, even on a comparatively large scale, is a measure of his confidence.

Lent by Mrs Sophia Mallin

73 The Goldfish Bowl
c.1900

Oil on canvas, 76.2 x 62.2 cm. (30 x 24½ ins.)

PROVENANCE: Purchased from Prof. Stockley; Gibson Bequest 1925.

LITERATURE: Sheehy, (1974), no. 546.

The girl with short hair is the painter's niece, Violet Stockley.

Lent by the Crawford Municipal Gallery, Emmet Place, Cork

74   The Lustre Jug
c.1901

Oil on canvas, 76 x 61 cm. (30 x 24 ins.)

Signed, bottom left: **Walter Osborne**

PROVENANCE: Purchased from the artist's executors, 1903. N.G.I. Cat. No. 553.

EXHIBITED: N.E.A.C., 1901, (77); R.H.A., 1902, (28), 45 gns; *Memorial Exhibition*, R.H.A., 1903-04, lent by the National Gallery of Ireland; *Ierse Schilders der 19e en 20e eeuw*, Stedelijk Museum, Amsterdam, 1951, (25).

LITERATURE: Sheehy, (1974), no. 558; *National Gallery of Ireland, 50 Irish Pictures*, (1983).

The children are the Reilly children from Portmarnock.[10] It is interesting that he should have gone back to the New English with paintings such as this, so very different in treatment (though not in subject) from his early naturalist work. This is much closer to the English 'impressionists' who came to dominate the club. It seems possible that Osborne had been looking at Monet, given the pre-occupation with light in this painting, and the variety of hues in the lit areas, and in the shadows — the tablecloth, for example.

Lent by the National Gallery of Ireland

75   The House Builders
1902

Watercolour, 47.7 x 59.8 cm. (19 x 23½ ins.)

Signed and dated, bottom left: **Walter Osborne 1902**

PROVENANCE: Purchased from the artist's executors, 1903. N.G.I. Cat. No. 2536.

EXHIBITED: N.E.A.C., Winter 1902, (14); *Memorial Exhibition,* R.H.A., 1903-04, (173), entitled *Building Card Houses,* lent by the National Gallery of Ireland.

LITERATURE: Sheehy, (1974), no. 571.

A domestic interior with children (possibly the Reilly children again) typical of the late work.

Lent by the National Gallery of Ireland

76   In the Garden, Castlewood Avenue *c.1901*

Oil on canvas, 50.8 x 61 cm: (20 x 24 ins.)

Signed, bottom left: **Walter Osborne**

EXHIBITED: Possibly *Under the Trees,*
Society of Oil Painters, 1901, (191), 50 gns;
probably, School of Art, Cork, 1935, *In the
Garden,* (67); *Paintings from Irish
Collections,* Hugh Lane Municipal Gallery of
Modern Art, Dublin, 1957, (166), lent by
John Burke.

LITERATURE: Sheehy, (1974), no. 555.

Painted in the garden at 5 Castlewood
Avenue, where Osborne continued to
live with his parents and his niece
(who may be one of the little girls in
pinafores) after his return to Ireland.
The picture is related to *Summertime*
exhibited at the R.A. in 1901, and
bought by the Corporation of Preston.

Private Collection

77   On the Beach *c.1900*

Oil on canvas, 59.7 x 73 cm. (23½ x 28¾ ins.)

PROVENANCE: Formerly collection of Mr. E. A. McGuire

EXHIBITED: There is a *Memorial Exhibition*, R.H.A., 1903-04, label on the back, but it is not clear under what title it was shown.

LITERATURE: Sheehy, (1974), no. 535.

This painting has bold, confident brushwork, and exceedingly daring colour — the mauve of the picnic-cloth, for example. It is very different in colour and handling from the early work, but it has the characteristic that we have seen in the *plein air* pictures of the eighties, of including figures as part of a scene, rather than as individuals. These figures are painted in such a way as not to be detachable, as figures in some of his early works were, from their environment.

Private Collection

78   Tea in the Garden *1902*

Oil on canvas, 132 x 217 cm. (54 x 67½ ins.)

PROVENANCE: Purchased from the
Trustees of Osborne's estate by Hugh Lane,
by whom presented, 1912.

EXHIBITED: *Memorial Exhibition*, R.H.A.,
1903-04, (116), entitled *Teatime*, lent by the
Trustees of Osborne's estate.

LITERATURE: Sheehy, (1974), no. 569.

Unfinished at Osborne's death April
1903, the picture was probably begun
the previous summer. A smaller
version (present whereabouts unknown) is inscribed, verso, 'Miss
Crawford 18, Miss Stockley 9, Castlewood Avenue'. The Crawfords lived
next door to the Osbornes; Miss
Crawford is the girl pouring tea; Violet
Stockley the child seated on the ground
looking out at the viewer; the figure on
the bench, barely sketched in, may be
the artist's mother Annie Jane
Osborne.

The painting is a combination of genre
and portrait, so much a feature of
Osborne's later work. It is on a larger
scale than usual, and correspondingly
more broadly handled. Though it is
regrettable that he did not finish it, it
does offer interesting evidence of the
way in which the painter laid in the
structure of a figure and built up the
modelling. It is much more painterly
than the earlier work, and less reliant
on preliminary drawing.

In subject and treatment the painting
is related to French Impressionism.
The sunlit outdoor scene recalls work
of Monet and Renoir in the seventies.
The palette, too, recalls Impressionist
experiments with light: look, for
example, at the range of colours in the
tablecloth and in the silver.

*Lent by the Hugh Lane Municipal
Gallery of Modern Art, Dublin*

79 George Clausen
(1852-1944)

The Haymaker, A Study in Shadows *1900*

Oil on canvas, 71.1 x 48.2 cm. (24 x 19 ins.)

Signed and dated, bottom right: **G. Clausen 1904.**

PROVENANCE: Presented by the artist, 1904.

This is a mature work of Clausen's, but shows his development to have had similarities to that of Osborne, who was also interested in the effect of sunlight falling through trees (Cat. Nos. 78 & 82). Like Osborne, Clausen has abandoned the 'square brush' of Bastien-Lepage, and has adopted a more varied handling.[11] The figure is more solidly modelled than we find in Osborne, and the brushwork coarser.

Lent by the Hugh Lane Municipal Gallery of Modern Art, Dublin

Portraits

Portraits

At the time of his death in 1903 Osborne was regarded as Ireland's leading portrait painter. A writer in *The Studio* observed that he had 'to the regret of his admirers deserted landscape for portraiture'.[1] AE wrote to Lady Gregory in 1901 'Dublin can't support more than one portrait painter — now it is Walter Osborne'.[2] He painted 'people of reputation, rank or fashion in Dublin'.[3] Both Stephen Gwynn and Thomas Bodkin, who knew him, maintain that he only turned to portrait painting out of a sense of duty when he had his family to support and his landscape genre scenes were not selling well: Gwynn quotes a poem of W. B. Yeats's about the stern laws of the Muse of poetry

> 'But never made a poorer song
> That you might have a heavier purse.'

and continues

> 'But what does the stern Muse lay down when, because somebody has to be looked after, a man feels himself called on to sacrifice his own artistic instinct, and even his preference for the less profitable way?'.[4]

Bodkin wrote, perhaps with some exaggeration

> 'Yet when seven years had passed without his being able to sell a single important landscape, he wrenched himself from what he truly loved and turned unflinchingly to what he thought was his duty.'[5]

Neither Bodkin nor Gwynn was a great admirer of his portraits. Bodkin[6] wrote that he was a thoroughly accomplished portrait painter, but that his landscapes had much more than accomplishment. Stephen Gwynn wrote that

> 'His work in portraiture, with all its technical dexterity, with all its charm of colour, lacked the essential gift. He could put breath into a landscape, he could give you the living atmosphere of a sky, but he could not make a human being live on canvas.[7]

> He was a little too courteous in the fibre of him ever to set down his impression of any other human being with entire unreserve.'[8]

138

There was, in fact, quite a lot of criticism of his portraits in his own time. Hilda Dowden, presenting her father's portrait to the National Gallery in 1916, wrote 'We do not consider this portrait a pleasing likeness . . .'[9] Sarah Purser was obviously a fierce defender of his work. Among her correspondence is a letter from Richard Colles, who seems to have incurred her displeasure by criticising Osborne:

'Dear Miss Purser,
I was very glad to get your letter this morning and learn that, whatever my as yet unknown fault may be, it is forgiven. If you refer to my having stated that W. Osborne is not very happy in his attempt to paint the portrait of the Chief Justice, I may as well say that it is the universal opinion so far as I can gather from persons known and unknown to me. [The portrait was of the Rt. Hon. Gerald FitzGibbon, Lord Justice of Appeal, exhibited at the R.H.A. in 1894 and again in 1895] .... But I have not seen the portrait by W. Osborne which may be said to be a success so far as portraiture in catching not alone the expression but the character of the individual is concerned. . . .'[10]

Analysis of the formal portraits does seem to bear out these judgements. Many of them, especially of men, are stiff, conventional and boring, and almost display the 'feelings of real distaste' with which Osborne is said to have approached them.[11]

This is especially true of the large commissioned portraits, like the one of the Chief Justice mentioned above. Another is *Sir Thomas Moffett* (N.G.I. Cat. No. 601, see frontispiece), a huge slab of official portraiture complete with Doctoral robes and the appurtenances of learning, or *Archbishop Plunket* (See House, Dublin), a posthumous portrait which looks it. On the other hand there are some magnificent portraits, and he did seem to be working his way into the genre. He had a great deal more success with women than with men. His portraits are more successful, too, when he was able to relax and paint friends and relations.

His portrait of *Miss Honor O'Brien* (Cat. No. 93) was much admired, and he himself believed he was at his best when he painted it. He painted a series of mothers and children, the most successful of which is *Mrs Noel Guinness and her Daughter Margaret* (Cat. No. 90), awarded a bronze medal in Paris in 1900, and much illustrated at the time. Of his portraits of friends his *Stephen Gwynn* (Cat. No. 80) and his *J.B.S. MacIlwaine* (Cat. No. 82) are rather different kinds of pictures, painted almost ten years apart, and both work very well. Children, too, brought out the best in him, as can be seen from *Master Arthur Stuart Bellingham and his Dog Dick* (Cat. No. 94) or the charming watercolour of his godson *Master Aubrey Gwynn* (Cat. No. 87).

In spite of the widespread idea that, by the end of his life Osborne was more of a portrait than a landscape painter, portraits, in fact, form quite a small proportion of his entire *oeuvre,* about sixty-six commissioned portraits out of a total documented output of about six hundred works, and only about one hundred portraits altogether. In 1895 only six out of forty-eight works were portraits, and though many of these were sketches and preparatory drawings he produced about five major works that year which were not portraits. In 1898, out of a total of thirty-three, five were portraits and eleven 'major' finished works. The impression that he was mainly a portrait painter was strengthened by the fact that he tended to send the portraits to major exhibitions such as the Royal Academy in London and the Royal Hibernian Academy in Dublin, and reserve his genre pictures for places like the New English Art Club.

Osborne's first commissions came at the end of the eighties — a group of works for the Pearsall family in 1888-9,[12] and from then on they grew steadily. Whether or not he was driven to portraiture for economic reasons, he began to exhibit an increasing interest in portraits by other painters, both contemporary and old-master. This could denote spontaneous interest or merely the professionalism that he brought to his work. Whistler he had always admired. In 1884 he did a tiny, precise drawing after the portrait of *Lady Archibald Campbell* at the Grosvenor Gallery, and he made two little drawings after Whistler at the Guildhall in 1896. He sketched *Miss Cicely Alexander* (Cat. No. 106) when it was shown in Dublin in 1899. The Dublin Sketching Club, of which he was, for a time, an active member, had a loan exhibition of twenty-six Whistlers in 1884 where Osborne would have seen the *Thomas Carlyle, Lady Meux,* and *Portrait of my Mother.* He gave a reproduction of the last painting to Stephen Gwynn, saying that it was a picture he loved.[13] It is difficult to pin down specific instances, but Whistler was clearly an influence on Osborne's portraits, though, unlike his landscapes, they rarely achieve the American painter's lightness of touch.

Orchardson was another painter whom Osborne admired, and who certainly influenced his portraits. There are striking similarities in both pose and treatment between Osborne's *Mrs Birdwood* (Cat. No. 85) and Orchardson's *Mrs Orchardson.* This last is reproduced in a monograph on Orchardson by Walter Armstrong that came out in 1895, the year that Osborne and Armstrong made their trip to Spain together. Armstrong may also have been a factor in Osborne's growing interest in old master portraits — notably in English painting of the eighteenth century, and in the work of Goya and Velázquez. The impact of the English is to be seen in his female portaits — there is a parallel between Reynolds' *Lady Betty Delmé and her Children,* which Osborne drew (Cat. No. 107) and his own groups of mothers and daughters. The Spanish painters reinforced his own feeling for tonal relationships, and subtle harmonies of colour, and helped his move towards increased freedom of handling.

By sheer concentration and professionalism Osborne asserted himself as Dublin's leading portrait painter. There was very little opposition — the only serious competition was John Butler Yeats, a better portraitist, though not as good a painter as Osborne, and he was hopelessly unprofessional, and could never reconcile himself to giving up a portrait until he had ruined it.[14] The two men could have done with a touch of each other's character. If Yeats had had some of Osborne's professionalism he would have been very successful indeed. And if Osborne had had more of Yeats's *laissez-faire* attitude towards his family we might have been spared the potboilers.

80   Stephen Gwynn *1885*＊

Oil on panel, 23.5 x 24.7 cm. (9¼ x 9¾ ins.)

PROVENANCE: Formerly collection of Mrs T. G. Moorehead, (daughter of the sitter).

EXHIBITED: *Memorial Exhibition,* 1903-04, R.H.A., (16), lent by Mrs Gwynn; *Great Irishmen,* Ulster Museum, Belfast, 1965, (87).

LITERATURE: Stephen Gwynn, *Garden Wisdom,* (1921). p. 34; Sheehy, (1974), no. 106.

Stephen Gwynn (1864-1950) was a lifelong friend of Osborne's. He came up as a Scholar to Brasenose College, Oxford, in 1882. He took a first in Mods. and Lit. Hum. 1884-86. He taught classics for a time, and later became a journalist and writer. He wrote of this picture:

'A genre picture rather than a portrait proper, it represents a very young man smoking a pipe while he reads, seen up against a studio table littered with brushes and palettes, and a wall roughly papered with sketches . . . I can date this work, for the book was Kant's *Ethics* which in 1885 I was reading for my degree'.

Lent by Mr. Terence de Vere White

＊Not exhibited in the Ulster Museum.

142

81 Sarah Purser *c.1890*

Pastel, 38.1 x 28 cm. (15 x 11 ins.)

Signed, bottom left: **Walter Osborne**

PROVENANCE: Formerly collection of the Purser family.

LITERATURE: Stephen Gwynn, *Garden Wisdom*, (1921), p. 34-5; Sheehy, (1974), addendum C.

Stephen Gwynn did not like this portrait:

> 'I think however, that this picture, for all its charm of composition and colour, does more justice to the grey teagown which the sitter had brought back from one of her visits to her old haunts in Paris than to the mordant intellectual power which made of Miss Sarah Purser a painter born to divine and portray character'.

Sarah Purser (1848-1943) was a cousin[15] of Osborne's. Obliged to earn her own living she decided to become a portrait painter, studying first at the Metropolitan School of Art in Dublin, and later at the Académie Julian in Paris. She was an effective and energetic force in the Dublin art world. She was seen by many as Osborne's successor in the role of Dublin's leading portrait painter 'it must certainly be your melancholy duty to finish his half begun portraits (being the only portrait painter left to us) you will be recognised as his heir (artistically)' wrote Hugh Lane shortly after Osborne's death.[16]

Private Collection

82   J. B. S. MacIlwaine
1892

Oil on canvas, 61 x 51 cm. (24 x 20 ins.)

Signed and dated, on tree, right: **W.F.O. -92.**

Inscribed, bottom right: *To my friend J. B. S. MacIlwaine 1892 Walter Osborne.*

PROVENANCE: J.B.S. MacIlwaine, from whom purchased, 1927. N.G.I. Cat. No. 882.

EXHIBITED: Dublin Arts Club, 1893, (104); *Centenary Exhibition,* National Gallery of Ireland, 1964, (182); *Aspects of Irish Art,* Colombus Gallery of Fine Arts, Toledo; Museum of Art, St. Louis Art Museum, 1974, (63).

LITERATURE: Sheehy, (1974), no. 341.

Osborne painted two portraits of MacIlwaine, one done in the schools of the R.H.A. when they were fellow pupils (Hugh Lane Municipal Gallery) and this one. MacIlwaine was a minor landscape painter, and a lifelong friend of Osborne's, who visited him often at his house at Foxrock, where this picture was almost certainly painted. It is one of Osborne's most successful male portraits, due to the combination of the *plein air* setting — the light falling dappled through the trees is particuarly effective — and the fact that the subject was a friend. The presence of the dog was probably also a help.

Lent by the National Gallery of Ireland

83   Self Portrait *1894*

Oil on canvas, 46 x 36 cm. (18½ x 14½ ins.)

Signed, top left: **Walter Osborne.**

PROVENANCE: Mrs. William Osborne, by
whom presented, 1903. N.G.I. Cat. No. 555.

EXHIBITED: *Memorial Exhibition,* R.H.A.,
1903-04, (67), lent by the National Gallery of
Ireland; *Great Irishmen,* Ulster Museum,
Belfast, 1964, (171).

LITERATURE: Strickland, (1913), p. 203, who
dates the picture, 1894; Stephen Gwynn,
Garden Wisdom, (1921), p. 38; Sheehy,
(1974), no. 393.

Stephen Gwynn wrote of this picture:
'Yet when I saw him last in his
studio in Stephen's Green his
aspect certainly lacked the un-
troubled vigour which one normally
associated with him. He looked
indeed much as he looks in the
picture of himself which, at Sir
Walter Armstrong's instance, he
had painted shortly before this for
the portrait collection in the
National Gallery of Ireland: thin,
his fresh colour concentrated on
the high cheekbones, now more
than ever prominent on the long
oval face . . .'.

Gwynn was mistaken in saying that
the picture was painted for the
National Gallery, since it was still in
the artist's studio at the time of his
death. The Manuscript Catalogue of
the National Gallery of Ireland states
that it was presented' by the artist's
mother in 1903.

Lent by the National Gallery of Ireland

84 Portraits *1894*

Oil on canvas, 50.8 x 61 cm. (20 x 24 ins.)

Signed and dated, bottom left: **Walter Osborne** -94.

PROVENANCE: Miss Violet Stockley, to the present owner by descent.

EXHIBITED: R.A., 1895, (631); Dublin Arts Club, 1895, (112); *Memorial Exhibition,* R.H.A., 1903-04, (142), lent by Mrs Osborne; School of Art, Cork, 1935, (66), called *At the Breakfast Table.*

LITERATURE: *Academy Notes,* (1895), from a drawing by the artist; Sheehy, (1974), No. 391.

This was painted at 5 Castlewood Avenue, and shows the painter's niece, Violet Stockley, in a high-chair. Walter Osborne's mother is seated by the child, and his father stands by the window at the back. It is an interesting instance, at a relatively early date, of the combination of portraiture and genre that we find in his last works.

Lent by Mrs Sophia Mallin

85   Mrs. Birdwood
1894

Oil on canvas, 90.2 x 69.8 cm. (35½ x 27½ ins.)

Signed, top left: **Walter Osborne**

PROVENANCE: Formerly collection of J.A.L. French Esq.

EXHIBITED: *Memorial Exhibition*, R.H.A., 1903-04, (123), lent by J.A.L. French.

LITERATURE: Sheehy, (1974), no. 394.

The sitter is Lucy, sister of W.F.P. Stockley, and was painted when she brought her baby niece home after her mother, Osborne's sister Violet died in childbirth. She is dressed in a travelling cloak and hat. It was painted in the autumn of 1894.[17]

Private Collection

86　Maude Gonne

Pencil on white paper, 22.9 x 15.2 cm. (9 x 6 ins.)

Signed and dated, top right: **Walter Osborne 1/11/95.**

PROVENANCE: Mrs Cecil Armstrong, by whom presented.

LITERATURE: Sheehy, (1974), no. 432.

Irish revolutionary heroine and abiding love of W.B. Yeats. Osborne did a large number of informal sketches of this kind, and he often captures the personality of the sitter in a way that his larger oils do not.

Lent by the Hugh Lane Municipal
Gallery of Modern Art, Dublin

87 Master Aubrey Gwynn *1896*

Watercolour, 29.9 x 24.2 cm. (11¾ x 9½ ins.)

Inscribed, bottom left: **To Mrs S. L. Gwynn from Walter Osborne**

PROVENANCE: Mrs. T. G. Moorehead, by whom presented, 1978. N.G.I. Cat. No. 7831.

EXHIBITED: *Irish Art in the 19th Century,* Crawford Art Gallery, Cork, 1971, (116).

LITERATURE: Sheehy, (1974), no. 471.

Stephen Gwynn's son, now Father Aubrey Gwynn S.J. He was Walter Osborne's godson. He later became Professor of Mediaeval History at University College, Dublin.

Lent by the National Gallery of Ireland

88   Mrs. Andrew Jameson and her Daughter Violet *c.1895-6*

Oil on canvas, 122 x 162.5 cm. (48 x 64 ins.)

Signed, top left: **Walter Osborne**

PROVENANCE: Andrew Jameson; formerly collection of Major Kirkwood.

EXHIBITED: R.A., 1896, (409); *Memorial Exhibition*, R.H.A., 1903-04, (104), lent by Andrew Jameson.

LITERATURE: *Royal Academy Pictures*, (1896); Sheehy, (1974), no. 467.

One of the earliest of Osborne's groups of mothers and daughters. It may owe something to Whistler — *At the Piano*[18] for example, but it doesn't manage to achieve Whistler's illusion of spontaneity. The composition is rather cluttered and the device of cutting off the chair on the right hand side is not entirely successful. The picture was apparently caricatured in *Punch* as *The Torture Chamber*.[19] Violet Jameson, playing the violin, was made to keep her pose by having her shoes nailed to the floor.

Private Collection

89   Sir Walter Armstrong *c.1896*

Oil on canvas, 98 x 80 cm. (37½ x 29½ ins.)

Signed, top left: **Walter Osborne.**

Inscribed, bottom left: *To my friend Walter Armstrong.*

PROVENANCE: Mrs Deas, (daughter of the sitter), by whom presented, 1959. N.G.I. Cat. No. 1389.

EXHIBITED: R.A., 1896, (369); *Memorial Exhibition,* R.H.A., 1903-04, (100), lent by Sir Walter Armstrong; *Irish International Exhibition,* Dublin, 1907, (74), lent by Sir Walter Armstrong; *Franco-British Exhibition,* Paris, 1908, (60), lent by Sir Walter Armstrong; *Exposition d'Art Irlandais,* Brussels, 1930, (123), lent by Major Armstrong.

LITERATURE: E. R. and J. Pennell, *Whistler,* (1911), p. 399; Sheehy, (1974), no. 472.

Sir Walter Armstrong (1850-1915) was Director of the National Gallery of Ireland 1892-1914, and was a close friend of Osborne. He was a distinguished art historian and critic.[20] The portrait was hung on the line at the Royal Academy. Whistler noticed it on a visit to Dublin in 1900, as Armstrong told the Pennells

> 'The only other remark on any particular picture which I can now recall is his saying of my own portrait by Walter Osborne, "It has a *skin,* it has a *skin!*"'.'

What Whistler may have meant by this is not at all clear.

Lent by the National Gallery of Ireland

90   Mrs Noel Guinness and her Daughter Margaret *1898*

Oil on canvas, 137.2 x 152.4 cm. (54 x 60 ins.)

Signed and dated, top left: **Walter Osborne** -98

PROVENANCE: Noel Guinness to the present owner by descent.

EXHIBITED: R.A., 1898, (597); R.H.A., 1899, (6); *Exposition Internationale*, Paris, 1900, awarded a bronze medal; *Memorial Exhibition*, R.H.A., 1903-04, (34), lent by Noel Guinness; Works of Irish Painters, Guildhall, London, 1904, (45); *Irish International Exhibition*, Dublin, 1907, (125), lent by Noel Guinness; *Exposition d'Art Irlandais*, Brussels, 1930, (116), lent by Noel Guinness.

LITERATURE: *Academy Notes*, 1898; *Royal Academy Pictures*, 1898; *Guildhall Exhibtion Catalogue*, 1904; *Great Pictures in Private Collections*, (1904); Sheehy, (1974), no. 511.

This is the most famous of all Osborne's commissioned portraits, and one of the most successful, perhaps because he was also on friendly terms with the sitter, for whom he painted a pair of little seascapes (Cat. No. 70).

Lent from the Guinness Collection

91   Mrs Noel Guinness and her Daughter Margaret — Sketch *c.1898*

Oil on canvas, 42.5 x 50.8 cm. (16⅞ x 20 ins.)

PROVENANCE: Noel Guinness, to the present
owner by descent.

LITERATURE: Sheehy, (1974), no. 512.

Sketch for Cat. No. 90.

Lent from the Guinness Collection

153

92   Mrs Noel Guinness and her Daughter Margaret — Sketch *c.1898*

Pen and ink, 24.7 x 21.5 cm. (9¾ x 8½ ins.)

PROVENANCE: Noel Guinness, to the present owner by descent.

The sketches for the large painting are an indication of the degree to which the panache it achieves is the result of careful preparation.

Lent from the Guinness Collection

93 Miss Honor O'Brien *c.1898*

Oil on canvas, oval, 68.6 x 50.8 cm. (27 x 20 ins.)

Signed, bottom left: **Walter Osborne.**

PROVENANCE: Rev. Lucius O'Brien; Miss Honor Crosbie (daughter of the sitter), to the present owner by descent.

EXHIBITED: R.A., 1898, (367); *Autumn Exhibition*, Walker Art Gallery, Liverpool, 1898, (20); R.H.A., 1899, (115); *International Exhibition*, Cork, 1902, lent by the artist; *Works of Irish Painters*, Guildhall, London, 1904, (182).

LITERATURE: Sheehy, (1974), no. 513.

The *Freemans Journal*, 7 December 1903, in its account of the *Memorial Exhibition* said 'He believed he was at his best in his portrait of Miss Honor O'Brien'.

Lent by Mr. J.R. Eyre-Maunsell

94 Master Arthur Stuart Bellingham and his dog Dick *c. 1898*

Oil on canvas, 59.7 x 49.5 cm. (23½ x 19½ ins.)

Signed, bottom left: **Walter Osborne.**

PROVENANCE: By descent.

EXHIBITED: R.H.A., 1898, (251); *Memorial Exhibition,* R.H.A., 1903-04, (7), lent by Mrs Bellingham.

LITERATURE: Sheehy, (1974), no. 509.

According to the sitter the dog wriggled and scratched a lot during the first sitting, and the painter ordered that he be de-flea'd before the next one.

Private Collection

95   Canon Travers Smith, DD. *1901*

Oil on canvas, 73.7 x 62.2 cm. (29 x 24½ ins.)

Signed, top left: **Walter Osborne.**

PROVENANCE: Vicar of the Church of St. Batholomew, Dublin.

EXHIBITED: R.H.A., 1902, (223); *Memorial Exhibition,* R.H.A., 1903-04, (93), lent by Canon Travers Smith; *Works of Irish Painters,* Guildhall, London, 1904, (26); *Church Disestablishment,* National Gallery of Ireland, 1970, (105).

LITERATURE: Sheehy, (1974), no. 564.

The parish magazine of St. Bartholomew's Church dates this at 1901 (see *Church Disestablishment,* 105, mentioned above). The liveliness of this portrait makes it an exception among Osborne's male portraits, and certainly among his clerical ones.

Lent by Rev. John Neill, Vicar of St. Bartholomew's.

96 Mrs Caesar Litton Falkiner — Sketch
c.1902

Oil on canvas, 55.9 x 43.2 cm. (22 x 17 ins.)

PROVENANCE: Miss E. Webb, by whom presented, 1948.

LITERATURE: Sheehy, (1974), no. 573.

This is a sketch for the large *Portrait of a Lady* in the National Gallery of Ireland (Cat. No. 1060).

Lent by the Limerick Municipal Art Gallery

97 John Hughes
R.H.A. *1902-3*

Watercolour, 60.8 x 46.5 cm. (23 x 17⅞ ins.)

Inscribed bottom left: *This is my portrait by Walter Osborne. One of the last pictures he painted. Presented by me to Lady Stoker, May 1903. John Hughes.*

PROVENANCE: Thornley Stoker, by whom bequeathed, 1912. N.G.I. Cat. No. 2668.

EXHIBITED: *Memorial Exhibition,* R.H.A., 1903-04, (180), lent by Lady Stoker; *Irish International Exhibition,* Dublin, 1907, (264), lent by Lady Stoker; Watercolour Society of Ireland Centenary, 1970, (108); *Drawings from the National Gallery of Ireland,* Wildenstein, London, New York, 1967, (28).

LITERATURE: Sheehy, (1974), no. 583.

The portrait shows the sculptor John Hughes (1865-1941) in his studio. The sculpture is his *Orpheus and Eurydice,* now in the Hugh Lane Municipal Gallery of Modern Art. The portrait is unfinished.

Lent by the National Gallery of Ireland

The Catalogues

The Catalogues

From 1884 Walter Osborne was an assiduous and, in the early days at least, conscientious, exhibition-goer. He bought, and often annotated, exhibition catalogues, and many of these have survived. When he died his mother presented them to the National Library of Ireland. They form an interesting guide to Osborne's attitude to painting, and to his changing taste over the years.[1]

Early in 1884 he visited the first *Winter Exhibition* of the Institute of Painters in Oil Colours, and covered the catalogue in pencilled notes. Two or three pictures were singled out for special attention; he considered that Clausen's *Daydreams* was

> 'By far the best picture in the exhibition. Splendid colour and tone in the old woman's head against a sunny field. The girl's grey dress also a wonderful piece of tone and execution. Very strong in colour. Pure chromium in the grass. Very rough texture of canvas, too much so in background'.

It is not surprising, given the direction of his own painting, that Osborne should have admired Clausen, and it is probable that the two painters knew each other. It is also interesting that he should comment on formal and technical matters. Occasionally in his notes, he notices subject matter, but usually his interest is that of one painter in the craft of another. A subject that did elicit his admiration was R.C. Woodville's *In the Nick of Time*. The catalogue illustrated a detail, against which the young Osborne wrote:

> 'A fragment of a really fine picture. Reminds one of de Neuville. Thinly painted but full of action. Represents three mounted soldiers coming down a steep embankment in haste to prevent some Egyptian troops from blowing up a bridge. Water in the foreground with two Egyptians and a laden mule coming towards you. First rate colour? action.'

He made a small sketch of the whole composition. In Alma-Tadema he admired that master's command of execution, remarking of *Well Known Footsteps*:

> 'A splendid piece of execution and colour. Note reflected light on woman's face from marble in sunlight. Woman

in grey purple dress. Cornelian necklace. Very rich and deep.'

Again one can see the admiration of one painter for the skill of a fellow artist. Bodkin[2] has suggested that Osborne was interested in anecdotal paintings, but what really emerges from a study of the catalogues is that his main interest was in the craft of painting, and he was prepared to admire it wherever he encountered it, however different the subject matter might be from his own. He was primarily interested in colour, and then in handling. He sometimes jotted down the colours in a picture, as he did in his preparatory drawings for paintings. He was also concerned with 'truth', something that ties him to the Realist tradition: W. L. Wyllie's *Black Diamonds* was 'a very true picture'; in Alfred Parsons' *The Daylight Dies* the water and foreground were 'very well painted and true'; Clausen's *Daydreams* was 'so real'. On the other hand J. L. Wood's *Abbeville* was 'a most detestable smoothly painted work. Looks like an amalgamation of two or three towns. Not a bit true.' Osborne's dislikes were as emphatic as his likes: *Klea,* by Edwin Long was 'a horrid smooth badly drawn work'. On the whole he praised 'strength', what he regarded as beautiful colour, 'cleverness', and often remarked that a picture was 'splendidly painted'. He criticised thin or smooth painting, and sometimes noticed if a picture was badly drawn. A pattern seems to emerge from his observations, that on the one hand he noted paintings which for one reason or another attracted his attention, and on the other hand he noted pictures by his friends and acquaintances. The way in which he marked some paintings suggests that he knew their author — Alma-Tadema and J. R. Reid are two painters about whom one gets this impression.

He visited the summer exhibition at the Grosvenor Gallery in May 1884, where similar tastes and preoccupations are apparent. J. R. Reid's *The Rival Grandfathers* was commented upon, with copious colour notes and qualified approval. Alfred Parsons was admired again, *Meadows by the Avon* 'one of the best landscapes in the Gallery. Very true effect of sunset'. There is some evidence of an interest in portraiture — he made a sketch after Alma-Tadema's *Portrait of Herr L. Lowenstam,* and a tiny, precise drawing after Whistler's *Lady Archibald Campbell.* He also admired Millais' *Marquess of Lorne,* but found Herkomer's

Portrait of Bird Foster, Esq. 'flashy', and *Mrs Legh* by Sargent 'flimsy'. He was still praising 'truth', 'strength', 'good colour' and broad handling. On the other hand he criticised paintings for being black, or 'hard and careful'.

The catalogues for the later period have far fewer annotations, but there are more sketches. This may indicate a shift in interest from handling and colour to composition. Osborne was now more interested in portraits and figure subjects, and less in landscape. His admiration for Alma-Tadema continued — at the New Gallery in 1893 his *Unconscious Rivals* was 'magnificent'. Waterhouse, too, attracted his attention, and Edwin Abbey's *Richard, Duke of Gloucester.* He went on noticing the work of old friends of the *plein air* school — Stott, Clausen, La Thangue, Fred Hall and Frank Bramley, but new names began to appear — Sargent, Abbey, Fred Brown, Wilson Steer. Among portrait painters he noticed work by Sargent quite often — his *Mrs Hugh Hammersley* at the New Gallery in 1893 was 'magnificent', and he did a sketch after a *Portrait of a Lady* at the Royal Academy in 1896. He also noticed portraits by Millais and Orchardson.

There are two catalogues of Loan Exhibitions, with a mixture of contemporary paintings and earlier ones, where Osborne's reactions are interesting. The first of these was at the Guildhall in 1896, where there was a loan collection of watercolours. He passed over the Turners, save one, but did notice some work by Cox and de Wint. The two other artists he selected particularly are, in different ways, very interesting. He made two small sketches after Whistler, sustaining an admiration he had expressed in the early catalogues. The other selection links him to a previous generation of rural genre painters — he noticed no less than three works by Fred Walker, reserving his particular admiration for *Philip in Church.* He made extensive colour notes, and admired the 'exquisite feeling'.

In 1899 he was on the committee of an Art Loan exhibition in Dublin organised by his friend Armstrong. It contained eighty-eight pictures 'by the best British and Continental artists', and aimed at 'the illustration of some of the main tendencies of painting during the last half century'. Osborne's copy of the catalogue is full of drawings, both in pencil and in ink, after Millais, Leighton, Millet, Orchardson and Whistler. The Millet he chose, *L'Amour Vainqueur,* a classical subject, is odd, given

Osborne's realist antecedents. It, and the Leighton, are the only two nudes in his entire oeuvre. Two other drawings are significant as indications of his shifting taste. Both are very fine —one, Whistler's *Cicely Alexander* is in pencil, the other, Orchardson's *Master Baby,* in pen and ink. The Orchardson is related to Osborne's own studies of women and children. A strong indication of Osborne's shift in taste is the fact that the exhibition was full of Barbizon, Hague School, and English Realist paintings, yet he chose figure paintings belonging to quite different traditions.

He visited other loan exhibitions at the Guildhall. In 1896 he made a couple of sketches after a Holbein portrait of Henry VIII. Perhaps he had in mind the increasing volume of commissions for portraits of men in court dress or judicial robes. In 1899 he sketched the composition of Reynold's *Lady Betty Delmé and her Children,* which was an interesting choice, considering the number of mother and daughter portraits he did towards the end of his life.

Another feature of the later catalogues is Osborne's growing interest in the portrait painting of Goya and Velázquez. Perhaps this can be attributed to the influence of Armstrong, who was an expert on Spanish painting, but it also seems to relate to something in Osborne's own work and the development of his taste. Armstrong was on the committee for the exhibiton of Spanish Art at the New Gallery in the winter of 1895-6. Osborne visited the exhibition, and did a lively little sketch after *Prince Baltazar Carlos in the Riding School,* attributed to Velázquez. He immersed himself even more thoroughly in Spanish painting at the Guildhall in 1901, though it is significant that in an exhibition that included lots of religious and genre subjects — Murillo, Zurbaran, El Greco — he mostly noticed the portraits, and only those by Goya and Velázquez.

The catalogues throw an interesting light on Osborne's character — his meticulousness, his thoroughness, and, occasionally, his sense of humour. Most of all they show a man with a conscientious approach to his profession. In the early catalogues we see him absorbing all he can of the skills of his craft. In the later ones, faced with new problems, he sets himself to explore systematically the varieties and possibilities of portrait painting.

98   Institute of Painters
in Oil Colours 1883-84

(161) *Day Dreams.* **GEORGE CLAUSEN**

Pencil notes, see page 162.

The painting is in a private collection.

99 Grosvenor Gallery, Summer Exhibition, *1884*

(192) *Portrait of Lady Archibald Campbell.*
J.M. WHISTLER

Pencil sketch, with dimensions 96 x 5 ½, right hand margin.

The painting is in the Philadelphia Museum of Art.

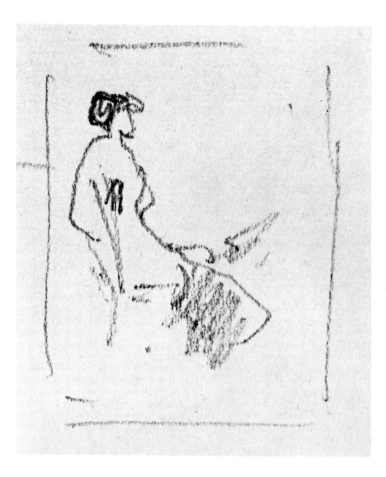

100   London
Corporation Art Gallery,
The Guildhall. Loan
Collection of
Watercolour Drawings,
1896.

a.   (101) *A Drawing.* **J. M. WHISTLER**

   (Lent by Arnold A. Hannay).

   Pencil sketch, right hand margin.

b.   (108) *A Drawing.* **J. M. WHISTLER**

   (Lent by Arnold A. Hannay).

   Pencil sketch, right hand margin.

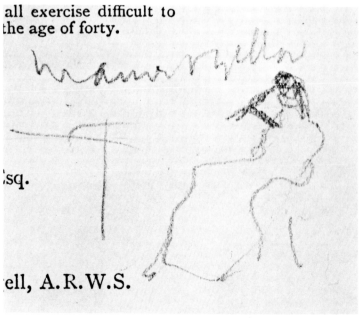

Lent by the Trustees of
the National Library of Ireland

168

101 New English Art Club, 10th Exhibition
1893

(3) *Design for a Fan.* **E. DEGAS**

Pencil sketch and note 'scheme in red and gold'

102 New English Art Club, 12th Exhibition *1894*

Sketch inside flyleaf, *A Lover of Art*

H. H. LA THANGUE.

232. THE WOODMAN.

H. S. TUKE.

233. PICKING CARNATIONS.

W. HOLMAN HUNT.

234. PORTRAIT OF HAROLD RATHBONE, ESQ.

C. E. PERUGINI.

235. FRAGRANT FLOWERS.

J. MACWHIRTER, R.A.

103 New Gallery, 7th Exhibition *1894*

(232) *The Woodman.* **H. H. LA THANGUE**

Pencil sketch and notes 'striking effect of evening sun on figures'.

104 New Gallery,
Exhibition of Spanish
Art *1895-6*

Inside flyleaf, sketch after *Prince Baltazar
Carlos in the Riding School,* (No. 59 in the
exhibition).

The painting is in the collection of the Duke
of Westminster, Grosvenor Estate.[5]

*Lent by the Trustees of
the National Library of Ireland*

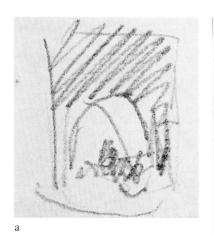

a

105 The Corporation of London Art Gallery, the Guildhall. Spanish School *1901*

a. (60) *Interior of a Prison.* **F. GOYA**

Pencil sketch.

The painting is in the Bowes Museum, Barnard Castle.

b. (66) *Portrait of the Painter's Brother.* **F. GOYA**

Pencil sketch and notes 'grey green background, plum coloured coat'

The painting is in the Bowes Museum, Barnard Castle, and is now thought to be Don Juan Antonio Meléndez Valdéz.

c. (120) *Prince Baltazar Carlos as a Hunter.* **VELÁZQUEZ**

Drawing, with colour note 'browns and greys'

The painting is in the collection of the National Trust and H. M. Treasury, Ickworth, and is now considered to be a studio work.

d. (131) *The Infanta Maria Teresa (?).* **VELÁZQUEZ**

Drawing

The painting is in the Metropolitan Museum, New York. The attribution to Velázquez is disputed, as is the identity of the sitter.

66. PORTRAIT OF THE PAINTER'S BROTHER.

By GOYA.
Canvas 29 × 21 ½ inches.
Lent by the TRUSTEES OF THE BOWES MUSEUM.

b

c

d

Lent by the Trustees of the National Library of Ireland

173

37. A Bather.
Lent by E. Onslow Ford, Esq., R.A.

a

b

c

106   Art Loan Exhibition, Dublin *1899*

a.   (37) *A Bather.* **LORD LEIGHTON**

Pencil sketch

b.   (49) *The Gambler's Wife.* **J. E. MILLAIS**

Pencil sketch in margin p. 36.

c.   (50) *Stella.* **J. E. MILLAIS**

Pencil sketch, tipped in.

d.   (51) *L'Amour Vainqueur.* **J-F. MILLET**

Pencil sketch in margin p. 37.

e.   (58) *Master Baby.* **W. Q. ORCHARDSON**

Pen and ink drawing p. 52.

The painting is in the National Gallery of Scotland, Edinburgh, and was once in the McCulloch Collection.¹

f.   (79) *Miss Cicely Alexander.* **J. M. WHISTLER**

Pencil sketch p. 57.

The painting is now in the Tate Gallery, London.

37

MILLET, JEAN FRANÇOIS.

BORN, 1814. DIED, 1875.

51

d

f

e

107   London
Corporation Art Gallery,
The Guildhall, *1899*
Turner and some of his
Contemporaries

(170) *Lady Betty Delmé and her Children*

Pencil sketch, p. 136.

Lent by the Trustees of
the National Library of Ireland.

Bibliography

Manuscript sources

Campbell, Julian, *Irish Artists in France and Belgium 1850-1914*. Ph.D. Thesis, University of Dublin, 1980.

Fletcher, W. T. Blandford, Notebook, mostly dealing with his student career, and early days painting in Belgium and England.

Osborne, Walter. Papers formerly in the possession of his niece, Miss Violet Stockley.

Purser, Sarah, Papers, National Library of Ireland, 10,201.

Royal Dublin Society, Minute Book of Taylor Competition, 1878 on.

Printed Sources

Académie Royale des Beaux Arts, Antwerp. *Rapports Annuels* 1881-90.

Armstrong, Walter, *The Art of W. Q. Orchardson*, (London, 1895).

Arnold, Bruce, *Orpen*, (London, 1981).

Artists of the Newlyn School. Exhibition, Newlyn, Plymouth, Bristol, 1979.

Benson, Rev. J. C., *Rathmines School Roll*, (Dublin, 1932).

Blackburn, Henry, *Breton Folk*, (London, 1880).

Bodkin, Thomas, *Four Irish Landscape Painters*, (Dublin, 1920).

Cartwright, Julia, *Jules Bastien-Lepage*, (London, 1894).

Sir George Clausen R.A., Exhibition Bradford, London, Bristol, Newcastle-upon-Tyne, 1980.

Crookshank, Anne and The Knight of Glin, *The Painters of Ireland*, (London, 1978).

Denson, Alan, *John Hughes*, (Kendal, 1969).

Norman and Alethea Garstin, Exhibition, Penwith, Bristol, Dublin, London, 1978.

Gregory, Augusta, Lady, *Hugh Lane's Life and Achievement*, (London, 1921).

Gwynn, Stephen, *Garden Wisdom*, (Dublin, 1921).

The Hague School, Exhibition, Paris, London, The Hague 1983.

Hartrick, A. S., *A Painter's Pilgrimage*, (Cambridge, 1939).

Irish Art in the 19th Century, Exhibition, Crawford Art Gallery, Cork, 1971.

Laidlay, W. J., *The Origin and First Two Years of the New English Art Club*, (London, 1907).

Mitchell, Susan, *George Moore*, (Dublin, 1916).

Moore, George, *Modern Painting*, (new edition, London, n.d.).

Moore, George, *Salve*, (London, 1912).

Murphy, William M., *Prodigal Father*, (Cornell University Press, 1978).

McConkey, Kenneth, 'The Bouguereau of the Naturalists', *Art History* I 3, 1978, pp. 371-82.

The McCulloch Collection of Modern Art, Winter Exhibition, Royal Academy, London, 1909.

Osborne, Charles, *The Life of Father Dolling*, (London, 1903).

The Peasant in French 19th Century Art, Exhibition, Douglas Hyde Gallery, Trinity College, Dublin, 1980.

Peasantries, Exhibition, Newcastle-upon-Tyne, Sheffield, Paisley, Aberdeen, 1981-2.

Pennell, E.R. & J. *The Life of James McNeill Whistler*, (London, 1911).

Pevsner, Nikolaus, *Academies of Art*, (New York, 1973).

Potterton, Homan, 'A Director with Discrimination', *Country Life*, May 9, 1974, pp. 1140-1141.

Post-Impressionism, Exhibition, Royal Academy, London, 1979-80.

The Restless Wave, Exhibition, Newcastle-upon-Tyne, 1978.

Ritchie, Alick P. F., 'The Antwerp School of Art', *The Studio*, I 1893, pp. 141-2.

Robinson, Lennox, *Palette and Plough*, (Dublin, 1948).

Sheehy, Jeanne, *Walter Osborne*, (Ballycotton, 1974).

Solvay, Lucien, *Le Paysage et les Paysagistes: Theodore Verstraete*, (Bruxelles, 1897).

Strickland, W. G., *A Dictionary of Irish Artists*, (Dublin and London, 1913).

Sutton, Denys, 'Sir Walter Armstrong', *Apollo*, CXV Feb. 1982.

Thaddeus, H. J., *Recollections of a Court Painter*, (London, 1912).

Theuriet, André, *Jules Bastien-Lepage and his Art*, (London, 1892).

Thornton, Alfred, *Fifty Years of the New English Art Club*, (London, 1935).

Verlat, Victoire & Charles, *Charles Verlat*, (Anvers, 1925).

Notes to the Text

Introduction

1. W. G. Strickland, *A Dictionary of Irish Artists,* (Dublin and London, 1913), Vol II, pp 201-7. Since the records of the Royal Hibernian Academy, and State Records held at the Four Courts, Dublin, were destroyed in 1916 and 1922 it has been necessary to rely on such sources as Strickland, Thomas Bodkin's essay in *Four Irish Landscape Painters,* (Dublin, 1920), and Stephen Gwynn's *Garden Wisdom,* (Dublin, 1921). All three men knew Osborne, so they are a useful and, on the whole, reliable source of information. For a more thoroughly annotated biography, and a *catalogue raisonné* of Osborne's work see Jeanne Sheehy, *Walter Osborne,* (Ballycotton, 1974).

2. Rev. J. C. Benson, *Rathmines School Roll 1858-99,* (Dublin, 1932). *Rathmines School Magazine* VI, 5 Sept. 1877.

3. For Burton see Homan Potterton, 'A Director with Discrimination', *Country Life,* May 9th, 1974. Burton's relationship to the Osbornes is referred to in a letter from Margaret Stokes to William Osborne, Purser Papers, National Library of Ireland, *MS*10201. The relationship was not a close one, and there is no evidence of the two men knowing each other, though it is very likely that they did meet when Osborne began to frequent London in the eighties.

4. *Rathmines School Magazine,* see above. *The Year's Art,* I 1880, p. 77, and II 1881, p. 80.

5. See Alan Denson *John Hughes,* (Kendal, 1969), pp. 33-4. The evidence quoted suggests that Osborne attended classes at the Metropolitan School 1877-1880. A letter dated 14/4/81 from the headmaster, Robert Edwin Lyne, inserted in the Taylor Competition Minute Books at the Royal Dublin Society, certifies that Walter Osborne was a pupil.

6. Taylor Competition Minute Book, RDS.

7. Nikolaus Pevsner, *Academies of Art,* (New York, 1973), p. 220 and *passim.*

8. The list of nationalities includes U.S.A., England, Austria, Bavaria, Egypt, Spain, France, Holland, Dutch East Indies, Italy, Prussia, Russia, Saxony, Sweden, Switzerland and Turkey, though out of all of these the significant numbers came from Holland, (an average of 66 a year 1875-84), England (an average of 27 a year 1875-84), France (an average of 11 a year 1875-84), and Prussia (an average of 14 a year 1875-84). The numbers from *Angleterre* were quite high in the late seventies (17 in 1875, 16 in 1876-7, 20 in 1878-9) but increased sharply to 35 in 1880, 38 in 1881, 43 in 1882, 37 in 1883 and 35 in 1884. *Académie Royale d'Anvers, Rapports Annuels,* 1881-1890.

9. *Sir George Clausen RA,* Exhibition, Bradford, London, Bristol and Newcastle-upon-Tyne, 1980. p. 15.

10. *Artists of the Newlyn School,* Exhibition, Newlyn, Plymouth, Bristol, 1979, p. 15. Also Registration Books, Royal Academy of Fine Arts, Antwerp.

11. *Artists of the Newlyn School, op. cit.* p. 163, and Registration Books, Antwerp Academy, *op. cit.*

12. Registration Books, Antwerp Academy, *op. cit. The Restless Wave,* Exhibition, Newcastle-upon-Tyne, 1978.

13. *Artists of the Newlyn School, op. cit.,* p. 15.

14. *Black and White. Handbook to the Royal Academy and New Gallery Exhibitions,* (1893), p. 8.

15. *The Studio,* I (1893), p. 142.

16. *idem.*

17. Julian Campbell, *Irish Artists in France and Belgium 1850-1914,* Ph.D. Thesis, Dublin University, 1980. For a full account of the Irish at Antwerp see Dr. Campbell, passim.

18. *Norman and Alethea Garstin,* Exhibition, Penwith, Bristol, Dublin, London, 1978. Registration Books, Antwerp Academy, *op. cit.*

19. Académie Royale d'Anvers, *Rapports Annuels, 1881-90.*

20. Victoire & Charles Verlat, *Charles Verlat,* (Anvers, 1925). It may be necessary to make some allowance for filial bias in their account.

21. The house no longer exists. There is continual tension between the French and Flemish languages in the Antwerp literature of the period. The Registration Books of the Academy, *op. cit.,* give the students' addresses in Flemish, though elsewhere, for example in the catalogues of the RHA, they are in French. Thus *Kloosterstraat* is sometimes given *Rue du Couvent,* and *Keizerstraat, Rue de l'Empereur.* Charles Verlat is sometimes spelt Karel Verlat, and the final t sounded.

22. *Baedeker's Belgium and Holland,* 1910. The Museum's Collection of paintings was still housed in the same building complex as the Academy.

23. Registration Books, *op. cit.*

24. Guidebook, *Stichting Nicolaas Rockox,* Antwerp. I am indebted to the Director, Dr. K. Vanderhoeght, for his help.

25. *The Complete Letters of Vincent van Gogh,* (London, 1958), II, p.472ff. Van Gogh was in Antwerp for a few months late in 1885 and early in 1886.

26. Lennox Robinson, *Palette and Plough,* (Dublin, 1948), p., 56. Alick Ritchie, *The Studio,* I 1893, p. 141-2.

27. Notebook in the possession of Miss Rosamund Fletcher, the painter's daughter, to whom I am indebted for allowing me to use it.

28. Catalogue, RHA 1882.

29. Henry Blackburn, *Breton Folk,* illus. by Randolph Caldecott, (London, 1880), p. 128-130, and p. 132.

30. Born Henry Thaddeus Jones (sometimes just Harry Jones), he reversed the order of his names and added a cubit to his stature.

31. H. Jones Thaddeus, *Recollections of a Court Painter,* (London, 1912), pp. 22-25.

32. Hill gave his address as *Maison Gloanic* (sic), Pont-Aven when he sent work to the Taylor Competition at the RDS in 1884. Since Hill and Osborne worked and travelled together, it seems likely that Osborne stayed there too. See also Blackburn, *op. cit.*

33. For the influence of Augustus Burke see Campbell, *op. cit.* In 1898 Osborne made a posthumous portrait of his brother, Thomas Henry Burke, who was murdered in the Phoenix Park in 1882.

34. Notebook, *loc. cit.* 'Trifle' Rowe was probably Tom Trythall Rowe.

35. *Sir George Clausen RA. op. cit.,* p. 29.

36. *Art Journal,* 1893, p. 169; *The Studio* IX, 163 and XXXV, 81.

37. Stephen Gwynn, *Garden Wisdom,* (Dublin, 1921), p. 32.

38. *Who was Who 1941-50,* (London, 1957).

39. Gwynn, *op. cit.,* p. 31.

40. Osborne to the Dublin Sketching Club and Burke to the RHA.

41. Letter, Purser Papers, *loc. cit.* 20/10201. "I used to see a great deal of him when he came to England, both in the country and in London, in fact the first time I met him I think was at Walberswick in the eighties. . . .'

42. *Post-Impressionism,* Exhibition, Royal Academy, London, 1979-80, p. 213. Most sources give Stott's date of birth as 1859. I am indebted to G. E. Thornber, Rochdale Public Libraries and Arts Services, for the information that the Register of Births, Rochdale has an entry for Edward William Stott, 25th April, 1855.

43. Letter formerly in the possession of Miss Violet Stockley, the painter's niece.

44. Notebook, *op. cit.* The drawing is in the possession of Miss Rosamund Fletcher.

45. Alfred Thorton, *Fifty Years of the New English Art Club,* (London, 1935), p. 3.

46. W. J. Laidley. *The Origin and First Two Years of the New English Art Club,* (London, 1907), p. 3.

47. George Moore, *Modern Painting,* (New Edition, London, nd.), p. 211.

48. Letter formerly in the possession of Miss Violet Stockley. It is only a fragment, but probably dates from 1884-5.

49. *Some Chantrey Favourites,* Exhibition, Royal Academy, 1981.

50. Strickland, *op. cit.* Vol. II, p. 202.

51. Quoted Alan Denson *op. cit.,* p. 68, par. 210.

52. Interview Lady Glenavy, née Beatrice Elvery, 1970.

53. J. Sheehy, *op. cit.,* p. 43.

54. Dublin Sketching Club Catalogues, Annual Exhibitions 1874-85.

55. E.R. & J. Pennell, *The Life of James McNeill Whistler,* (London, 1911), p. 239, quoting a letter from W. Booth Pearsall, Hon. Sec.

56. Francis Bate, *The Naturalistic School of Painting,* (2nd Edition, London, 1887). Registration Books, Antwerp Academy, *op. cit.*

57. Catalogues, Dublin Arts Club 1886-92. Amalgamated with the Instrumental Music Club and became Dublin Arts Club, 1893.

58. Strickland, *op. cit.,* p. 202.

59. Gwynn, *op. cit.,* p. 36-7.

60. *Ibid.,* p. 34.

61. *Idem.*

62. Letter, dated Bordeaux 5th December 1895, Purser Papers, *loc. cit.* 10201.

63. For example *Freeman's Journal* 7/12/1903, "Thereafter he went to Paris. . . ."

64. Letter to Sarah Purser, *loc. cit.*

65. Denys Sutton, 'Sir Walter Armstrong', *Apollo* CXV, 240, Feb. 1982, pp. 72-75.

66. Walter Armstrong, Walter Osborne, in DNB 1901-1911, p. 55.

67. George Moore, *Salve,* (London, 1912), pp. 159 & 363.

68. Sir Hugh Lane to Sarah Purser 13/5/1903, Purser papers *loc. cit.*

69. J. Sheehy, *op. cit.,* p. 53.

70. Bodkin, *op. cit.,* p. 38.

71. Bruce Arnold, *Orpen,* (London, 1981), p. 37. Sheehy, *op. cit.* Catalogue Nos. 338 and 540.

72. Letter, undated, from Miss E. Webb to Miss Violet

Stockley. Formerly in Miss Stockley's possession.

73. On Jane Austen's principle 'It is a truth universally acknowledged, that a single man in possession of a good fortune, must be in want of a wife' Osborne's name, like that of Hugh Lane, was constantly being linked with that of one woman or another, though it seems likely that Osborne, unlike Lane, would have married had circumstances allowed. Lady Glenavy's (interviewed 1970) explanation was that he 'had a mother', Lady Hanson's (also interviewed 1970. She was Deena Tyrrell, and painted by Osborne 1902-3) that he had sacrificed himself for his parents and his niece.

74. Bodkin, *op. cit.*, p. 38.

75. Gwynn, *op. cit.*, p. 31.

76. Susan Mitchell, *George Moore*, (Dublin, 1916), p. 90.

77. Gwynn, *op. cit.*, p. 32.

78. Interview, see Note 52.

79. Gwynn, *op. cit.*, p. 32.

80. Bodkin, *op. cit.*, p. 38.

81. Strickland, *op. cit.*, p. 203. It is not clear why he declined. Bodkin *op. cit.*, p. 37 suggests modesty. His niece said that he found it difficult to entertain at home, and that this might have deterred him. She also suggested that he might have refused it because of the sort of people to whom knighthoods were being given.

82. The Medal was in the possession of the painter's niece. See also *Art Journal*, special edition devoted to the *Exposition Internationale*, 1900.

Early Work: Antwerp and Brittany

1. Letter, dated 1872, formerly in the possession of the painter's niece.

2. V. & C. Verlat, *op. cit.*, p. 53. The painting now hangs in the *Zaal Karel Verlat* at Antwerp Zoo.

3. V. & C. Verlat, *op. cit.*, p. 53.

4. *Ibid.*, p. 55.

5. Académie Royale, *Rapport Annuel*, 1883. There were 26 people in the class.

6. V. & C. Verlat, *op. cit.*, p. 81.

7. *The Complete Letters of Vincent Van Gogh, op. cit.*, pp. 475ff.

8. *Norman and Alethea Garstin, op. cit.*, p. 19.

9. Lucien Solvay, *Le Paysage et les Paysagistes: Theodore Verstraete*, (Bruxelles, 1897), p. 68.

10. Exhibition catalogue, *The Hague School*, Paris, London, The Hague, 1983.

11. *Ibid.*, p. 33.

12. *Ibid.*, p. 16 and *passim*.

13. It is possible that these influences permeated to Dublin. There does not seem to be any direct connection with the Hague School, except that H. W. Mesdag exhibited at the R.H.A. in 1876, but between 1876 and 1886 there are quite a number of views of places like Dordrecht and Scheveningen exhibited by such Irish marine painters as Edwin Hayes, Nathaniel Hone and W. Booth Pearsall.

14. V. & C. Verlat, *op. cit.*, p. 55.

15. A. S. Hartrick, *A Painter's Pilgrimage*, (Cambridge, 1939), p. 28.

16. *Idem.*

17. R. Jope-Slade. 'The Outsiders', *Black and White*, 1893, p. 11

18. André Theuriet, *Jules Bastien-Lepage and his Art*, (London, 1892), p. 77.

19. Notebook, *loc. cit.*

20. This painting has always been referred to as *Modenke Verhoft*. Dr. Guido Persoons, Librarian at the Koninklijke Academie Voor Schone Kunsten, Antwerp, suggests that it should be *Moderke*, "little mother".

21. *The Hague School, op. cit.*, p. 187ff.

22. *Ibid.*, p. 201ff.

Plein Air Painting in England

1. For discussion of Bastien's influence in Britain see Kenneth McConkey, The Bouguereau of the Naturalists, *Art History* I 3, 1978, pp. 371-382.

2. Julia Cartwright, 'Jules Bastien-Lepage,' *The Portfolio*, (London, 1894), p. 17.

3. Gwynn, *op. cit.*, p. 43-4.

4. Letter, undated, but probably 1884-5, formerly in the possession of Miss Violet Stockley.

5. Hartrick, *op. cit.*, p. 28.

6. Theuriet, *op. cit.*, p. 66.

7. Letter from North Littleton, October 12th 1884, formerly in the collection of Miss Violet Stockley.

8. Burke exhibited work from Walberswick at the RHA in 1884.

9. See *Post-Impressionism, op. cit.*, p. 204 (327).

10. Letter 2/10/84 from North Littleton, *loc. cit.*

11. See *The McCulloch Collection of Modern Art*, Royal Academy Winter Exhibition, 1909. Special Number of *The Art Journal*.

12. In the autumn of 1885, Stott gave his address as Wherwell nr. Andover.

13. The drawing is in the possession of Miss Rosamund Fletcher.

14. *The Irish Revival* exhibition catalogue, Pymm's Gallery, London, 1982, says that the I.P.O.C. label is on the back.

15. Once in the McCulloch Coll. Now Aberdeen Art Gallery.

16. Once in the McCulloch Coll. Now National Gallery of Victoria, Melbourne.

17. Gwynn, *op. cit.,* p. 30.

Ireland, Landscape and Genre

1. For a discussion of French Rural Genre see *The Peasant in French 19th Century Art*, Douglas Hyde Gallery, (Trinity College, Dublin, 1980).

2. Letter from Steer to Sarah Purser, nd. *loc. cit.*

3. *Moonrise,* lent to Art Loan Exhibition, Dublin, 1899.

4. Letter to Sarah Purser dated 5/12/1895, *loc. cit.* It is quoted in full, Sheehy, *op. cit.,* pp. 37-40.

5. Brian Fallon. 'Osborne Revisited', *Irish Times,* 11th May 1974, who suggests that I regard Osborne as a precursor of Impressionism'. I do not, and never did. It would be absurd to say this of a painter whose earliest works date from the eighties. One does not need to take an 'evolutionary' view of art to suggest that Osborne was influenced by Impressionism, or that his later work has more power and expression than his earlier.

6. Homan Potterton. *Irish Church Monuments,* (Belfast, 1975), p. 44.

7. Letter to Sarah Purser 13/5/03, *loc. cit.*

8. Letter to Sarah Purser, see note 4. Jeremy Wood has pointed out that Armstrong's *Velazquez* (London 1896) contains a drawing by Osborne after *Mercury and Argus* in the Prado, Madrid.

9. According to Miss Violet Stockley. A letter to her, dated August 15th (1901) is addressed from Hill Cottage, St. Marnock's Malahide.

10. According to his niece, Violet Stockley.

11. *Sir George Clausen R.A.,* p. 67.

Portraits

1. *The Studio,* April 1897, p. 257.

2. Lady Gregory, *Hugh Lane's Life and Achievement,* (London, 1921), p. 35.

3. Bodkin, *op. cit.,* p. 34.

4. Gwynn, *op. cit.,* pp. 29-30.

5. Bodkin, *op. cit.,* p. 35.

6. *Ibid.,* p. 29.

7. Gwynn, *op. cit.,* p. 38.

8. *Ibid.,* p. 42.

9. File on this portrait, Library, National Gallery of Ireland.

10. Letter 5/3/95, *loc. cit.*

11. Bodkin, *op. cit.,* p. 34.

12. W. Booth Pearsall was Hon. Sec. of the Dublin Sketching Club. He was an amateur (?) marine painter, and exhibited at the RHA. There are some marine panels by him set in the plasterwork of the hall of the Royal Irish Yacht Club, Dun Laoghaire.

13. Gwynn, *op. cit.,* p. 33.

14. For an exhaustive account of J.B. Yeats see William M. Murphy, *Prodigal Father,* (Cornell University Press, 1978).

15. There are several references to the relationship among Sarah Purser's Papers, *loc. cit.*

16. Letter 13/5/1903, *loc. cit.*

17. According to Miss Violet Stockley, niece of both the painter and the sitter.

18. Now in the Taft Museum, Cincinnati, Ohio.

19. I have not succeeded in tracing it.

20. Denys Sutton, *op. cit.*

The Catalogues

1. For a complete list of the annotated catalogues see Sheehy, *op. cit.,* pp. 159-161.

2. Bodkin, *Four Irish Landscape Painters,* Dublin, 1920.

3. I am indebted to Jeremy Wood for notes on the Spanish Paintings sketched by Osborne.

4. *The McCulloch Collection of Modern Art,* Royal Academy Winter Exhibition, 1909.

Index

Index of Lenders